PRAISE FOR DEVI BROWN AND *CRYSTAL BLISS*

"From the instant you meet Devi, she gives off a calming, yet positive and infectious, energy."

—*The Cut* for *New York* magazine

*

"Brown is introducing millennials to a version of spirituality that doesn't intimidate or boast, but instead...meets them right where they are."

—*Her Agenda* (www.HerAgenda.com)

*

"The Houston radio personality launched Karma Bliss to spread mindfulness, meditation, and the power of crystals to a stressed-out world."

—*Houstonia* magazine

*

"While there are many who talk the good energy talk, Brown is a testament to the fulfillment that accompanies knowledge of oneself and desire for continuous growth."

—*xoNecole* (www.xoNecole.com)

PRAISE FOR DEVI BROWN AND *CRYSTAL BLISS*

"The first word that comes to mind when thinking about Devi Brown is energy. She resonates a positive energy that is not just experienced through meeting her in person but also when you listen to her on the radio or watch her on television."

—*TheGrio* (www.theGrio.com)

✳

"Devi Brown is known for getting some of the biggest names in hip-hop—Kendrick Lamar, Big Sean, and Nicki Minaj, to name a few—to open up about their personal struggles. Now she's sharing her journey from music to meditation (she's a certified teacher!), getting real about building a business and showing everyone how to find their own 'bliss.'"

—Essence.com

✳

"Devi's passion for helping others find mindfulness and fulfillment in their lives manifests itself in amazing ways through all of the self-discovery methods in which she specializes—including crystal healing. Her expertise and relatable writing style will take you on a life-changing journey not only toward your own self-discovery, but toward finding a deeper connection to others and to the world we live in."

—Taylor Behrendt, producer for America's number one national morning TV show

CRYSTAL *Bliss*

ATTRACT LOVE.
FEED YOUR SPIRIT.
Manifest Your Dreams.

DEVI BROWN

Adams Media

New York   London   Toronto   Sydney   New Delhi

Adams Media
An Imprint of Simon & Schuster, Inc.
57 Littlefield Street
Avon, Massachusetts 02322

First Adams Media hardcover edition OCTOBER 2017.

ADAMS MEDIA and colophon are trademarks of Simon and Schuster.

For information about special discounts for bulk purchases, please contact Simon & Schuster Special Sales at 1-866-506-1949 or business@simonandschuster.com.

The Simon & Schuster Speakers Bureau can bring authors to your live event. For more information or to book an event contact the Simon & Schuster Speakers Bureau at 1-866-248-3049 or visit our website at www.simonspeakers.com.

Interior design by Colleen Cunningham
Crystal illustration by Claudia Wolf
Chakra illustration by Eric Andrews

Manufactured in the United States of America

10 9 8 7 6 5 4 3 2 1

Library of Congress Cataloging-in-Publication Data
Brown, Devi, author.
Crystal bliss / Devi Brown.
Avon, Massachusetts: Adams Media, 2017.
Includes bibliographical references and index.
LCCN 2017026418 (print) | LCCN 2017027691 (ebook) | ISBN 9781507202609 (hc) | ISBN 9781507202616 (ebook)
LCSH: Crystals--Therapeutic use. | Self-care, Health. | BISAC: BODY, MIND & SPIRIT / Crystals. | BODY, MIND & SPIRIT / Healing / General. | SELF-HELP / Spiritual.
LCC RZ415 (ebook) | LCC RZ415 .B76 2017 (print) | DDC 615.8/52--dc23
LC record available at https://lccn.loc.gov/2017026418

ISBN 978-1-5072-0260-9
ISBN 978-1-5072-0261-6 (ebook)

Contains material adapted from the following title published by Adams Media, an Imprint of Simon & Schuster, Inc.: *The Encyclopedia of Crystals, Herbs, & New Age Elements* by Adams Media, copyright © 2016, ISBN 978-1-4405-9109-9.

Dedicated to

my supportive and funny husband, DUANE,

our crazy fur babies, LEGEND and ALI,

and ALL THOSE who are looking to add

more meaning to their lives.

ACKNOWLEDGMENTS

A huge thank you to YOU for picking up this book and adding some crystal energy into your life. Whether this is a complement to a practice you already have or your first visit into the world of higher consciousness, I am so grateful that you are moving forward into the deeper parts of yourself and taking me along for the ride.

Thank you to my gorgeously handsome husband, Duane, for the constant love, transparency, support, laughter, and encouragement. Thank you to my friend Linda Walsh for gifting me with my first piece of citrine all those years ago; that beautiful gesture gave me hope in a time when I desperately needed my broken spirit to be healed. Thank you to the Chopra Center and Chopra Center certifications for showing me how to return to wholeness and inspiring me to live my life more fully and with more intentional impact. Jeremy, the most amazing soul consultant ever, thank you for the many healing hugs. The Goddess known as Jennifer, thank you for your healing hands, patient ear, and beautiful heart! My brother and business manager Humble Lukanga for helping me view myself without limits and for always reminding me what a blessing being alive is! Thank you Rebecca Tarr (!!), Laura Daly, and all of Adams Media/Simon & Schuster for your guidance, patience, and this incredible opportunity to share myself in such a big and lasting way. Thank you to my fabulous family—Mom, Auntie Doreen, and Darren—for unconditionally loving me and showing me a world full of culture, beauty, and opportunity from the first moment I was born. Thank you to my extended family—Myra and Dennis Brown, Grandma Flo, and Lamont and Marlene

Gooding for the support and love. My brother Charlemagne, thank you for being yourself in such a big way. Deeply wise, beaming with brilliance, and impossibly ratchet. From the moment we met you have been one of my truest friends, a constant supporter, and one of my biggest inspirations. Thank you to my friend and former PD Adrian Scott for always challenging me and sharing your wisdom every chance you got. Thank you to my iHeartmedia radio family—Doc Wynter, Eddie Martiny, Marc Sherman, Michael Saunders, Tutu Durant, Lisa Baldon, Rudy Rush, DJ Mr. Rogers, Zelma, and Shante. Thank you to those whose full lives have served as my guideposts and whose work has deeply inspired me and led me to a greater understanding of myself—Oprah Winfrey, Frida Kahlo, Tupac Shakur, Deepak Chopra, Elizabeth Lesser, Kendrick Lamar, ScHoolboy Q, J. Cole, Lauryn Hill, Ms. Dynamite, Malcolm X, Martin Luther King Jr., Barack Obama, and Joel Osteen. Thank you to Ila Singleton, Vanessa Anderson, April Bombai Pongtratic, Mari Ronquillo, Erica Dumas, Brianne Pinns, Marlene Meraz, Ret One, Punch, John and Aventer Gray, Romina Foster, Brooke Adibe, Joanna Simkin, Terrace Martin, Bad Lucc, Tracy G, Necole Kane, Mar Brown (RIP—you will be missed forever), Rabia Ilahi, Erin Garza, Tara Hasselbarth, Candy Shaw, Sabrina McKnight, Jarrod McClain, Monique Hobbs, Christine K, Bun B and Queenie Freeman, Aaron Drake, Charles Dorsey, Heidi Lukanga, Folasade Ayangibile, Denise Hamilton, Joy Sewing, Tiffany Willams, and all the rest of my incredibly supportive tribe of friends who always have my back and my heart.

JOIN OUR KARMA GANG

When I launched Karma Bliss in the summer of 2016, my goal was to demystify ancient Vedic teachings and get them into the hands of people who were living how I once had...stressed out, consumed with consuming, and disconnected from the truest parts of themselves. There were four specific ways I reprogrammed my spirit: meditation, crystal healing, journaling, and vision planning. Karma Gang is made up of the people who have come on this journey with me in search of more joy, peace, and meaning in our daily lives. They're the folks who are giving themselves their best effort. The seekers. Join the movement by connecting with us on social media and checking out the website!

* www.KarmaBliss.com
* Facebook.com/KarmaBlissed
* Instagram.com/KarmaBlissed

You can also connect with me on my personal site, DeviBrown.com, and please tag me with any thoughts or pictures at @DeviBrown on *Twitter*, *Facebook*, and *Instagram*!

CONTENTS

Part One.
Getting Started with Crystals ✧ 19

Part Two.
Crystals for Specific Uses ◆ 63

Chapter 5. Crystals for Creativity 77

Chapter 6. Crystals for a Happy Home 89

Chapter 7. Crystals for Love and Relationships 101

Part Three.
Furthering Your Crystal Journey ◇ 167

INTRODUCTION

My love affair with crystals began when I was around ten years old. I had gotten a small leather pouch filled with colorful tumbled stones while on a field trip. Each day that summer, I'd find time to sit in my room and pour them out of their bag and onto the floor. I would admire their vibrant colors and run my fingers over their smooth textures. I didn't know why I was so fascinated by them, but I loved the way they made me feel. It's interesting to look back at the things that tugged at you as a child, in the time before we knew the stress and disconnected lifestyles that awaited us. It is often those same childhood hobbies that are the keys to expanding our peace and growth as adults.

A little over a decade later, I was a twentysomething excelling in the radio and entertainment industry. Primarily working in hip-hop, I was living a pretty enviable lifestyle that included interviews with big-name celebs, invites to exclusive events, and all-access passes to amazing concerts. To most, I was "living the life," but in reality, I had become a stress addict, and I had a gnawing, empty feeling inside that fun could no longer fill. I was longing for a deeper understanding of my purpose, and I was physically exhausted. A trip to the hospital after a stress-induced illness came with doctor's orders to find new ways to unload and relax. Thus began my journey into meditation and a re-sparked love affair with crystals, which eventually led me to become a certified teacher of primordial sound meditation and a guide to crystals and self-discovery.

My first life-changing experience with crystals came after a girlfriend gifted me with a beautiful citrine pendant. At the time, I was grieving an extreme loss in my life and was in the process of figuring out the next move to make in my career. She told me the stone would guide me, so I gripped it tightly in my hands and visualized all the ways I wanted it to help me transform my life, both personally and professionally. I wore it to sleep, in the shower, while working out…it never left my side. Then, when I finally wore out its chain, I started tucking it into my bra and wearing it next to my heart. (Obsessed? Definitely.)

From the moment I set my focus on the crystal that first day, I noticed shifts happening all throughout my life. I experienced enhanced mental clarity, opportunities I desired began manifesting more easily and rapidly, and I began to have a greater sense of my purpose and a better understanding of how to tap into it. I was hooked and I wanted more.

From that point forward, these ancient, magical, natural resources became a part of my everyday life. I've since traveled the world collecting them, hiding them in every crevice of my home, and even started a business, Karma Bliss, built around connecting other people to them.

If you incorporate crystals into your life, you, too, will experience big shifts. Whether your goals are emotional, physical, financial, and/or spiritual, there is a specific crystal that can aid you in manifesting it. Stones like mookaite jasper or citrine can be powerful allies in your work life, bringing you enhanced creativity and charisma, while smoky quartz or chrysoprase can bring peace and tranquility to your living space. If attracting love or emotional healing speak to your inner needs, rose quartz or lapis lazuli are just what you are seeking, as they foster truthful communication and accelerate your ability to release what no longer serves you. In this book you will learn exactly why crystals are so powerful, how to start using them, and which ones can unlock the potential in your professional, home, and spiritual life.

So, let's get started. Welcome to the therapeutic, beautiful, and blissfully addictive world of crystals!

Part One

GETTING STARTED WITH CRYSTALS

Diving into the world of crystals can be overwhelming. Should you display them in your home or wear them? Are smooth, polished stones any more effective than the raw kind? How do you clean them? In the next few chapters I will reveal the history behind crystals, information on how to buy, use, and care for them, and I'll even give you a fast pass to starting your collection. Take a deep breath and get ready for the crystal turn up!

1.

What Is the Deal with Crystals?

Crystals are old. Really, really old. I'm talking anywhere from thousands to hundreds of millions of years old. The earth's age is estimated at around 4.5 billion years old, and some zircon crystals that were recently found in Australia were dated as being 4.4 billion years old. Pretty mind-blowing, right? Many scientists now believe that the earth's inner core is actually made up of an aggregate of small crystals. So, if crystals had eyes or ears… imagine what they would have seen and heard over their lifetime!

TAPPING INTO ENERGY USING CRYSTALS

While crystals are beautiful and make for excellent jewelry, there's a lot more to them. Though rocks, stones, and crystals appear to be just inanimate objects, they are actually energetic entities. These ancient gemstones have an amazing ability to help connect you to the energy of the universe. The energy of the universe is in all things that the earth creates. Our bodies get energy from food and water. Our homes can be powered with wind and sun. Even our spirits are led by an unseen energy that we feel pulsing through us. Crystals, like everything else in this world, retain the vibrations of the earth as well. Energy and wisdom from the beginning of existence resides inside every stone. We are able to harness that energy for ourselves by wearing crystals, holding them, placing them in our homes, and even carrying them with us. Their energy aids us in transforming ourselves mentally, physically, emotionally, and spiritually.

Everything in our universe, including us, is made up of matter and energy. I saw a post on *Instagram* recently that said, "Men lie, women lie, energy doesn't." And even though that post was overly simplified and kind of passive aggressive (you just know it was posted for an ex to see, right?), there was still a lot of truth to it. In fact, energy is the *universal* truth. It expresses the present moment honestly, and it can guide you where people and words cannot.

Crystal energy is able to work through our human energy system (through seven points on the body known as *chakras*) and our auras to manifest things in our physical bodies, environment, and in the spirit realm. Chakras are considered to be invisible energy wheels that form a straight line beginning at the base of our spines and going up to the top of our heads.

An aura is the unseen atmospheric energy that is generated by and hovers around every living thing. The sacred energy of crystals is very real, and using it to align ourselves with these types of energies can be a life-changing experience.

WHERE DO CRYSTALS COME FROM?

Crystals can be found all over our planet. They were formed in the earth's surface millions or even billions of years ago, typically during periods of shifting and change. In the modern western world we tend to focus our attention on around 200 different crystals, but in fact there are thousands of them, with new discoveries being made every day.

Crystals are found throughout the globe, in countries such as India, China, Mexico, Morocco, Peru…the list goes on and on. Some types of crystals, like quartz, can be found in multiple parts of the world while others are only sourced in one place, like the mookaite jasper of Australia or the Herkimer diamond found in upstate New York.

Most crystals and gemstones fall into one of three different categories: igneous, sedimentary, or metamorphic. The conditions that create each category of rock are quite different (molten lava for some, flowing water or heat for others), but typically two things are needed to form crystals: time and lots of pressure. The process of how a crystal is formed in the earth might have a big impact on the whether the flow of its energy is slow and steady or fast and dramatic. Agate, for instance, a stone that is extremely abundant and comes in thousands of varieties, is known to have a slow-building energy effect, often subtly working on the background issues of a person's life. On the other hand, moldavite, a meteorite that is often used as an amplifier stone, has an effect so intense that some people have broken into a cold sweat and even passed out when holding it.

While on a crystal hunt in Sedona a few years ago, I encountered a piece of moldavite on a necklace that left me dizzy when I held it in my hands. (Of course, being the extremist that I am, I bought it immediately.) Luckily, the kind woman I got it from saved me from myself by giving me strict directions on how to use it, warning me when not to (apparently it will give you nightmares if you sleep with it on). Now I use it sparingly, and only in specific instances when I am looking to manifest major change.

A RAINBOW OF COLORS

Aside from their powerful energy, one of the things that has always drawn me and many others to crystals is their naturally vibrant color variations. While I tend to be drawn to vivid greens and brightly hued pinks (these shades typically help open the heart and enhance success), crystals come in all sorts of colors. Calming blue, raging red, beaming yellow, and warming orange, to name a small few. The colors of healing crystals span the rainbow and are based on the chemical elements involved while the crystal is forming.

They come in different shapes and sizes, too, with each type of crystal carrying its own energetic properties and benefits, as well as its own specific atomic makeup.

WHY ARE HUMANS DRAWN TO CRYSTALS?

We know from ancient drawings and artifacts that humans have been using crystals for at least 5,000 years:

* Shamans and healers use crystals for spiritual, physical, emotional, and mental healing.
* Kings and queens wear them as adornments and use them for protection.
* Scientists have even found them useful as transmitters for information in the form of microchips.
* Watchmakers use quartz to keep time. Because of its precise frequency standard, quartz is able to help regulate the movement of timepieces.

There is a scientific reason why, since the dawn of humanity, we humans have found ourselves drawn to the beauty and energy of crystals. All of the energy in the universe vibrates at one frequency at another. This vibration is very subtle—most of us don't even feel it. Because crystals are made of the earth itself, they carry a unique kind of earthly energy. Their vibrations are happening at an extremely high frequency.

In physics there is something called the law of entrainment, or the universal law of resonance. This is the synchronization of frequencies between at least two energy sources. As humans, we operate at a lower and slower vibrational frequency than crystals do. So according to the law of entrainment, when two objects that have different vibrational rates become close to one another, the object that vibrates lower (us) gets drawn into the higher vibrational rate of the other (crystals). So our attraction to crystals is not just some New Age juju talk; it's physics.

As you begin to build your crystal collection, you will notice that you tend to be pulled toward specific crystals. That's this vibrational frequency balance at work. If you feel drawn to a crystal, it's likely one you *need* in your life. A friend once asked me to pick up a crystal for her on my next adventure. I quizzed her on what type of energy she was looking to invite into her life, and she could not think of anything specific—only that it be red. As I walked into one of my favorite crystal shops in San Diego, I was instantly drawn toward a small red cylinder-shaped crystal. As it turns out, this was a beautiful piece of rose-red rhodochrosite, a crystal known to help heal victims of abuse by amplifying their feelings of personal power and giving them courage to face the truth about their situation with loving awareness. My friend did not know how to share the traumas of her past with me, but energetically I was drawn toward the crystal that she needed for her journey.

So many people I have come across in the crystal community have shared similar stories of finding themselves literally pulled to a crystal and then finding out its healing properties were exactly what they needed. Energy is powerful. Sometimes it shows itself in dramatic fashion, but mostly, we subtly attract the energy that our subconscious needs. That's why I cannot stress it enough: when you are on a spiritual journey and doing self-work, you must stay open to all possibilities. Go with the flow and follow the energy.

CRYSTALS BRING CONNECTION

When you find the right stones for you, their energy will work in harmony with yours to enhance your life and reveal things that have been out of reach.

CONNECT TO YOUR GOALS

I don't think it's a coincidence that crystals are now making an appearance in the everyday lives of many modern cultures. Between being glued to our phones and social media feeds all day and the ever-changing political climate, we are all subconsciously yearning to connect a little deeper with one another and to be one with the earth and its vast wisdom. Crystals are amazing conduits of energy that can be used to accelerate your discovery of the things you are searching for—health, success, love, creativity, and so on.

CONNECT TO YOUR SPIRIT

Just like certain cures for things that ail us can be found in various plants, the earth is filled with crystals that we were meant to utilize for the betterment of our lives. If you believe in a higher power, one that watches over us and has equipped us with food and water as nourishment to sustain life and grow our bodies, doesn't it make sense that the higher power would also supply us with a way to help us nourish our spirits and grow our awareness? Crystals are food for our spirits, just like plants are food for our bodies. Using crystals, you can start tapping into that sacred earth energy, which, as I have learned from personal experience, will leave you more deeply connected to your inner self than you ever imagined possible.

CONNECT TO YOUR INTUITION

The energy of crystals is not only a way to commune with nature; it's also a way to connect with your higher power and a way to get in tune with the deepest parts of yourself. A few years ago, I was dowsing (a ritual where you ask a question and depending on which way a crystal swings, you are given a yes or no answer) with a smoky quartz pendant. It occurred to me after I got the answer that nothing was being revealed to me that I did not already—on some deep level—know. The magic of the crystal lies in that it will amplify your intuition and connect you to parts of yourself that you have buried behind a lifetime of programming, experiences, reasoning, and fear.

CONNECT TO YOUR SPIRITUALITY

Crystals are often used as an addition to existing belief systems, not as a replacement. You might use crystals in meditations between official services to connect to your spirituality. My personal belief system is God-based and I see crystals as parts of nature that were given multiple uses for our benefit.

TELLING OTHERS ABOUT YOUR CRYSTAL WORK

When I first started working with crystal energy, I got mixed reactions from the people in my life when I told them. They were either extremely intrigued and wanted in on the experience, or they thought I had lost my mind and was worshiping rocks all day. Crystal healing is not idol worship nor is it some type of magic trick. Crystal healing is simply utilizing the sacred energy of these 100 percent natural elements to grow your life's potential.

How you choose to activate your personal journey doesn't have to be something done in public, so feel free to go the route of keeping your daily practices intimate and personal. You don't need to broadcast your crystal use to everyone in your life if you don't want to.

Personally, I welcome the opportunity to share information, though I am sure to remain detached from any expectation of how it will be received. Others have the right to think of you and your beliefs as they wish and can choose to not engage in the same things as you do. I've found that if someone is greeting you with hostility, arrogance, or condescension, they have already committed themselves to misunderstanding you, and there is no reason to continue the dialogue. If you think you might know people who would enjoy using crystals too, you might consider telling them about your practice. Giving crystals as gifts to the people in your life tends to do the explaining for you as the recipients experience their energy for themselves! Much of what you learn in this book will equip you with answers to many of the FAQ you will start to get once people find out you are utilizing the ancient power of crystal healing.

2.

How to Use Your Crystals

Now that you have some background on why exactly crystals are so powerful, it's time to figure out how they can fit into your lifestyle. In this chapter, you will learn where you can place crystals around you, what purposes they might serve, and how to keep their power flowing through you for your highest good. And because it's important to use crystals respectfully and tune them to your unique vibrational frequency, you will also learn how to best cleanse, activate, and recharge your crystal collection. Aside from setting intentions on your crystals, mantras and affirmations can be powerful allies for manifesting healing and opportunity in your life. You'll add those tools to your spiritual toolbox in this chapter too. So, let's dive into some of the best ways to get you started using your crystals!

CRYSTAL USES

Crystals can be used in a multitude of ways! In ancient times stones were crushed into a fine powder and used as high-powered makeup, watchmakers have used quartz to help keep time, and scientists have utilized crystals to build lasers and microchips. In this chapter, we will go over specific ways to harness the healing power of crystals in your modern, busy, and hyperconnected, day-to-day life.

IN THE HOME

Nowadays our homes have a lot of competing energies in them. From air pollution to excessive amounts of electricity, to the chemicals we use to keep them clean—our homes are constantly subjected to a barrage of influences that can change the dynamic of the space. When used in the home correctly, crystals can be a powerful ally in keeping you protected from negativity and harmful environmental energy.

At this point, every corner of my home is filled with crystal energy. Even my backyard has a few stones buried in it. Each time friends come over, people comment that they love how my house makes them feel. Or they describe its "good energy." I take a lot of pride in that and always feel great about coming home.

It's important to really feel out your space and decide what the needs of your home are. Start by meditating on that thought or journaling about it and then begin to cleanse and clear your space before adding in the stones of your choosing. This ritual can be useful at your place of work as well, and the same process applies. Starting in Chapter 4, we will get more into which stones go where, but in the meantime, here are some ways that crystals can change your home's atmosphere.

As Décor

I love using crystals in my home because along with changing its energetic makeup, they also bring a lot of beauty to any room. Your crystals can add meaningful and eye-catching flair throughout your space. A favorite fast and gorgeous trick of mine is placing similarly colored crystals in inexpensive glass bowls and using them as centerpieces on my coffee table and in the dining room. A dear girlfriend of mine, genius jeweler Kimberly McDonald, has an incredible new home collection that incorporates her signature geode and precious stone designs into rugs, elegant mirrors, flatware, barware, and much more. I've noticed department stores have even begun carrying items like vanity boxes and serving bowls that are made with raw and tumbled crystals. They can coordinate with almost any design theme.

It's also easy to go the DIY route, like I do, using stones you already have in your collection. A quick search on Pinterest will have you overflowing with ideas and instructions. (After a trip to the power tools department in Home Depot, I've gone as far as to turn some of my favorite quartz pieces into knobs for my bathroom cabinets!)

To Create a Welcoming Environment

Crystals like iolite, chrysocolla, or topaz can be used in your home to liven up the atmosphere and help manifest a more social environment where parties and deep connection fill the room.

To Keep Away Unwanted Guests

Certain crystals can also help protect your home from visitors you'd rather not have. After placing raw stones like black tourmaline or rainbow obsidian near my front door, people who did not wish me well or who had a shady agenda either stopped coming by or would not seem to be able to spend any real time inside, usually claiming something had come up and they had to leave. Even door-to-door solicitors stopped ringing my bell!

To Invite Love

If you need more love and romance in the home (and c'mon, who can't use a little extra sprinkle of that?), put some rose quartz or merlinite crystals in the bedroom to get that type of energy flowing.

To Protect Yourself from Electromagnetic Emissions

When used in the home, crystals like hematite, black tourmaline, and lepidolite can even help shield you from the electromagnetic emissions that seep out of the electronics and gadgets that you have. Ferromagnetic (iron-containing stones like pyrite), piezoelectric (crystals in the quartz family that are naturally electrically charged and can produce a voltage when pressurized), and pyroelectric (crystals like quartz and tourmaline that can transform energy when heated or cooled) stones should be used when you're seeking protection from these emissions. So keeping one near the TV in the living room or next to your bed where you keep your cell phone (for that late-night scroll session) can aid in blocking out that harmful energy.

WORN AS JEWELRY

Now that you have begun to learn about crystal energy, it's pretty apparent why for centuries people have been obsessed with beautiful crystal jewelry:

* Diamonds are known as symbols of love (prized for their intensity and light energy).
* Royal crowns are covered in colorful gemstones. (It's no surprise that crystals like amethyst, ruby, and sapphire—known to enhance wisdom, intuitive energy, and their connection to the crown chakra—were used to create a "crown"...get it?)
* Various rings and necklaces are made of their wearers' birthstone. (Hello, star children!)

Somewhere in history, we forgot that the reason crystals were turned into jewelry wasn't just because of their beauty, but because our ancestors wanted to harness their energy while wearing them to manifest their desires. I believe that finding a way to wear crystals in my daily life is essential. A friend of mine even refers to the tiger's eye and onyx bracelets he wears as his "armor" and won't leave the house without them on.

Jewelry Options

There are many different types of jewelry that are commonly worn today: pendants, bangles, boho necklaces, malas, rings, bracelets, chokers, earing studs or hoops, ear laces, headdresses, anklets, toe rings, nose rings, belly rings, tongue rings, watches, and much, much more. Crystals can be incorporated in any of those.

Style

Utilizing crystal energy in your accessories doesn't have to mean that you're dripping in diamonds and fine jewelry either. You can choose one or two subtle items if that's more in line with your personal preferences.

I personally love the look and feel of raw stones (stones with a rougher texture, tumbled or cut and polished) as pendants or crystal malas (a meditation tool) wrapped five times around the wrist in place of bangles. My personal essentials, or "armor" that I'm rarely caught without, include a clear quartz point pendant (a gorgeous piece I call "the Goddess Necklace" and sell on KarmaBliss.com) and a large chrysoprase cocktail ring that I picked up while at a charity event. These two pieces speak to my need for more clarity and focus in my work life (clear quartz) and a deep desire to understand karmic patterns in my personal life (chrysoprase). I've found that not only do I feel better when I wear them, but I also attract an audience of people who want to know more about them.

The Goddess Necklace especially is a piece that, when I wear it, I have to swat stranger's hands away from when they walk up and try to touch it. They, like me...are drawn to its energy in a way that cannot fully be explained.

Cost

When it comes to crystal jewelry, prices can range anywhere from ninety-nine cents up into the millions of dollars. The price difference is based solely on aesthetics; how difficult it is to source them; and how much effort was put into cutting, polishing, or tumbling them. The cost has no correlation whatsoever to the power of the energy in the crystal. We are the ones who consider value in terms of monetary amounts; energy, on the other hand, does not place a price tag on itself. The important thing when choosing to build your crystal jewelry collection is to find what speaks to you and rock it (no pun intended) with pride.

FOR BEAUTY

Crystals can even be used in the beauty realm. Cosmetic chemists readily put crystal powders in beauty potions, tonics, and face creams that are sold at drugstores and department store counters around the world. Crystal-centered beauty brands like Sjal Skincare highlight the crystals in their products for energetic reasons. Many companies in general used crushed-up pearl for its iridescence. Some brands like Nurse Jamie now make crystal-based beauty tools, such as tourmaline face rollers. Cleopatra herself was said to have crushed pieces of lapis lazuli into a fine powder and used it as eye shadow, both for its beautiful blue color and its ability to elevate its wearers to a higher state of consciousness. Pretty amazing, right? From ancient Egypt to your vanity at home, crystal healing has been holding it down for ages.

FOR PHYSICAL HEALING

Mention of crystal healing has been found in Vedic texts from India and medical writings from China dating as far back as around 5,000 years ago. And though ancient uses and practices spanning millennia are a hell of a testament to their power, there is an even easier way to understand how and why crystals are tools for healing. Healing power is found in crystals because they are conduits of energy (and we are talking *millions* of years of energy). This allows them to enhance, hold, and share energy in ways that can provide physical and spiritual healing.

Utilizing crystals in these ways can have a profound effect on your mind, body, and soul.

Though no scientific research exists to support this type of ritual, crystal healing has spanned history and been used by many cultural groups. Most notably, the Chinese have utilized beautiful jade for its healing properties for thousands of years, and the Vedic healers of India have included crystals in pastes and elixirs as part of their Ayurveda practice. Today you can seek out and experience crystal healing from many energy workers, Reiki masters, and massage therapists in your area. Using crystals on your physical body for healing is something you can also do at home by yourself simply by placing crystals on different points, like the forehead or abdomen, and laying still for several minutes.

How Physical Crystal Healing Works

When you are new to the world of crystals, hearing the term "crystal healing" can be a little, well...weird. Images of gurus on mountaintops using crystals on altars or a white light shooting out of your body when you touch them may start to come to mind. Let me set you straight. In its most common use, physical healing using crystals refers to an alternative-medicine energy practice where a teacher or guide places crystals on specific parts of your body to draw out ailments and negative energy and improve your health in some way. They might:

* Put certain crystals on a body part that is ailing.
* Align crystals on your seven chakras (there's more on chakras in Chapter 14).

* Create crystal "grid" patterns on your body that enhance and direct crystal energy where it is needed or desired.

The vibrational frequency of the crystals' energy is used to recalibrate and adjust your energy dynamic in a way that will relieve pain and alleviate stressors.

What Ailments Can Crystals Heal?

Though traditional scientists won't validate the healing powers of crystals, you can try them and decide for yourself. Crystals have been widely said to have the power to speed up the healing process for injuries and even the common cold. (Carnelian is a great tool for this.) Common uses for physical crystal healing include depression, anxiety, migraines, menstrual cramps, muscle pain, arthritis, sexual dysfunction, back pain, and allergies.

The first time I experienced a Reiki healing with crystals, I was completely blown away. It was truly an out-of-body experience. At the time I was dealing with severe anxiety and fatigue, but I left the room with a feeling of immense peace, buoyant energy, and a heightened awareness of my inner self.

In Chapters 9–11, I will share some of my favorite stones that can be used to enhance physical, mental, and emotional health.

It's funny, you know how when you buy a new car, you all of a sudden start to see that same make and model everywhere? Well, once I became awake to the world of crystal healing, I started to notice their use in places I had not paid attention to before. Like the tourmaline face roller my facialist had been using on me, or the sauna at my favorite Korean bathhouse that was tiled floor to ceiling with jade because of its water-balancing qualities.

FOR SPIRITUAL HEALING

How Spiritual Crystal Healing Works

Work done with crystals for spirituality is on a subtle level, and can help to heal all kinds of brokenness. Crystals will help connect you to a sacred energy that can help you move forward in your journey toward balance and happiness.

What Can Crystals Help Treat Spiritually?

Common uses for spiritual crystal healing include crises of confidence, difficulty letting go of the past, fear, grief, a lack of self-worth, and addiction.

In the past couple of years, my good friend Rabia Ilahi, an expert family/couples and teen therapist in Houston, decided to add chakra energy healing to her practice and has noticed a big shift happening in her regular clients. Energy healing can often work at a deeper and quicker level than traditional talk therapy alone. When used together, her clients reported uncovering deeply rooted traumas, thoughts, and beliefs that have blocked their emotional, physical, and psychic progress. These blocks are often not known on a conscious level and may take years of traditional therapy/counseling to uncover. Some of Rabia's clients have wept uncontrollably on the table during healings, had visions or seen colors, experienced a divine energy that allowed them to develop their own spiritual gifts and talents, and many have felt deeply rested and more grounded, which has helped them pursue their lives with more success and confidence as the days and weeks continued.

A few of the crystals that Rabia keeps around her Dharma-Wellness practice include amethyst (for divine energy), fluorite and rose quartz (for their connection to the heart chakra), and Herkimer diamond (used as a tool to activate her own crown chakra before doing her healing work).

OPEN YOURSELF TO THE POSSIBILITIES

In my life, and in this book, I define crystal healing as a personal practice where you work with crystals as a way to improve your life—mind, body, and soul. But as you start your journey, please remember, crystal healing is not magic—at least not in the Harry Potter sense. It's not some quick fix to get all the cool things that you want. Crystals are powerful tools for accelerating and manifesting soul lessons, internal needs, and even your deepest desires.

I have personally experienced accelerated emotional healing from crystal use (remember my citrine pendant from the Introduction?) and even the spontaneous arrival of a career opportunity or random good luck has happened when I had my aventurine stone in my pocket. The secret to activating crystal healing in your life is to simply find the crystals that are right for you and stay open to the possibilities.

HOW TO CLEANSE YOUR CRYSTALS

Since crystals are conduits of energy and intentions, it is important to cleanse your new finds and rid them of any previous intent. You never know who had them before you or what they did with them! There are many ways to do this, but these three methods are my favorite and what I have known to be the most powerful.

USE SALT

Salt water is an incredible ancient purifier found in nature. Its natural antiseptic properties have long been used by healers, and even my own mother used it as a wellness tool, having me gargle with it when I was sick. (No, it didn't taste too good, but I felt better!) This method is pretty simple—all you need is sea salt; purified alkaline water or spring water; a glass bowl; and a few measuring cups/spoons. Here's what to do:

1. Add a half tablespoon of sea salt to every cup of water and give it a few stirs until it starts to dissolve. Gently add crystals to the mixture, making sure that they are fully submerged.
2. Close your eyes and, with hands hovering over the bowl, set the intention for the salted water to remove any negative energy from your crystals. (See "How to Activate Your Crystals" for more information on intentions.)
3. Gently add your crystals to the water and let them sit for a few hours or overnight. Then remove the crystals and rinse with purified alkaline water or spring water and pat dry.

I have also known people to skip the use of water and pack their crystals in bowls filled with only sea salt as a way to cleanse them. This method works fine if you happen to have large bags of salt handy; if not, go with the water-based directions instead.

Some crystals like lapis, opal, carnelian, turquoise, selenite, labradorite, malachite, and calcite should *not* be cleansed with salt water because they are either too porous or have metal properties, and the salt could affect their appearance or make them disintegrate altogether.

SMUDGE

Smudging, or giving your crystals a smoke bath, is another way to cleanse your crystals. This ancient practice revolves around using the smoke of bundled herbs as an energy purifier. Smudging your crystals with a sage bundle, palo santo wood, or incense is a great way to save on time.

Here's how to smudge your crystals:

1. If you are clearing the energy of one crystal, you may simply hold it in your hand as you do this. If clearing multiple crystals, it will be easier to put them in a small bowl or keep them close together on a table.

2. Use a match or lighter to light your sage bundle/palo santo wood until it smolders (NOT flames) and slowly wave the smoke back and forth over your crystals. I like to engulf my crystals with the smoke by passing it over every inch and angle of each crystal.

3. Once you have finished, simply stamp the embers out in the same fashion you would put a cigar out. An abalone shell is a popular accessory to use for this purpose while smudging as it provides a flame-resistant surface to put out your sage/wood, and it can be a catch-all for ash.

Sage smudging bundles are pretty easy to find these days at retailers like Whole Foods. Palo santo wood can be a little trickier to find, but most New Age stores should have it in stock. After a trip to Tulum, Mexico, this past winter, I fell in love with the smell and feel of copal incense (made from a resin found in copal trees) and have been using that for smudging as of late. You can find that in stick and rock form in specialty shops or through a quick search on Amazon.

The awesome bonus to using this method for crystal cleansing is that it gives off a very earthy and grounding smell. Plus, the cleansing power of the smoke will do more than just clear the energy in your stones—it will also clear your energy, as well as the energy in the room you are in too!

USE A SINGING BOWL

Singing bowls have been used for centuries all over the world for sacred rituals. Dating back thousands of years and originating in Asia, singing bowls are actually considered to be a "standing bell" because they rest flat on the ground and emit sound when their rim is struck. Singing bowls are wonderful tools for all sorts of energy work that are practiced today by healers, therapists, and even spas.

By far, using the vibrational, sacred sound of a singing bowl is my favorite method for crystal cleansing! This is the method I currently use to cleanse all of the products and crystals we feature on KarmaBliss.com before they go in the mail. You can use traditional Tibetan metal bowls that come with wooden mallets or quartz singing bowls (I have a small collection of these at home) with suede-wrapped mallets. Here's what to do:

1. Place the crystals close to the bowl (or in some cases underneath it) and begin by lightly striking the rim of the bowl three times (think of the sound as "ding...ding...ding") and then gliding the mallet around the outer rim of the bowl repeatedly.
2. Move the mallet in a full circle around the bowl's rim at a comfortable pace. Not too fast and not too slow. The sound will start faintly and then increase and grow to be more intense as you continue.

This process is an incredible way to clear out stagnant or negative energy, and it can be very powerful for your mind, body, and spirit as it also aligns your chakras. The sound feels very primal and lends itself to a very sacred and tranquil energy.

HOW TO ACTIVATE YOUR CRYSTALS

Okay, now that all the hard work of cleansing your crystals is done, we can get to the fun and transformative part!

Setting an intention is the most important part of your relationship with your crystal. An intention is when you state clearly and deliberately the desired outcome you are looking to experience in your life. A few examples can include: healing of heartache, forgiving those who have harmed you, finding purpose, creating financial abundance, or attracting love.

You should set an intention for each crystal individually so as to connect your needs and desires with their individual properties. I believe it is important to take a few moments to meditate while holding each crystal, before you set your intention, to allow your subtle level of consciousness to connect with the crystal's energy and let your intuition guide you to your authentic intentions. To activate your crystals with your intentions, follow these steps:

1. Start by sitting comfortably as you inhale and exhale deeply through your nose.
2. Introduce the question "What do I really want?" to the stillness and silence you have created. It's important to know that you are not trying to force yourself to come up with specific answers during this meditation. Rather, you are asking the question of the universe so that its answers will flow through you.
3. Sit and contemplate the answers to that question for about three to five minutes.

Once you have finished the meditation, gently open your eyes and follow the next set of steps.

1. REMOVE PREVIOUSLY SET INTENTIONS

The journey of a crystal is a long one. It has passed through many hands and environments while on its travels from deep within the earth to your hands. This doesn't mean that it's necessarily harboring bad energy or intentions, but part of a crystal's makeup is to retain energy. So nonetheless, it's holding on to lots of energy it encountered before it met you. This is especially true if it was found in a crystal shop where many people may have picked it up before you or if it was given to you by someone else.

Technically, you have already cleansed and cleared your crystal by following the directions in the previous section, but it doesn't hurt to do a separate ritual to remove any previously set intentions or energy from it.

1. Start by closing your eyes as you hold the crystal in your hands.
2. Next, visualize white light pouring into it. (I usually imagine it as a beam of light coming down from the sky and into my hands.)
3. As you do this, say, "I remove any previously set intention and all previous cords of connection from this crystal" aloud. I say this only once, but if you feel so led, you can repeat this a few times as you continue to visualize the white light.

2. PROGRAM YOUR CRYSTAL

Having removed any and all previously set intentions, continue to hold your crystal in your hands. If you have opened your eyes, gently close them and once again envision white light beaming into your crystal. Now you will say, "The intention I am setting on this healing crystal is _____. I will use its beautiful energy to grow my highest self." Be sure to be thoughtful and specific as you do this. Repeat this gently but deliberately three times.

If you feel so led, continue to hold it in your hands as you meditate on visions of the best possible outcomes for your life coming directly to you.

Your crystal now holds your specific intention and will work with the energy of the universe to help you manifest it in your life.

RECHARGE YOUR CRYSTALS

Remembering to recharge your crystals is just as important as cleansing them and setting your intentions. Think of it like this: what comes from nature will always long to return to nature. Keeping crystals in our homes or in our purses 24/7 disconnects them from their sources: soil and sunlight. Much like phones need to be charged and we need to sleep and eat to operate successfully, a crystal's energy will start to fade if it doesn't get to soak up a few rays every once in a while.

Typically, I recharge my crystals once a month by using both sunlight and moonlight. Once you get in the habit of doing this, you will be able to sense when your crystals need some extra TLC. As you begin, once a month is a good rule of thumb. The intention you set stays with your crystal unless cleared and cleansed of it. Here are your options:

USE THE SUN

The power of the sun is unmatched. It nourishes and warms all living things. I always joke with people that I myself am solar-powered and can only work and thrive when the sun is shining bright. Giving your crystals a sun bath is one way to keep them charged up. It's best to do this during clear weather, and it is as simple as gathering your collection together on a tray or plate and placing them in direct sunlight. I like to do all of my collection at once versus one at a time, but go with whatever feels best for you. You can place them on any convenient steps, balconies, windowsills, or other flat outdoor surfaces. You can place them almost anywhere as long as you make sure that they are in direct sunlight.

Leave the crystals outside all day if possible. If you find yourself crunched for time, I recommend a minimum of five hours. I will usually take them outside in the morning on the way to work and then bring them inside at the end of my day.

USE THE MOON

Seen as the feminine face of God by many belief systems, the moon has played a pivotal role in the evolution of earth and humanity. Much closer to us than the sun, the moon's gravitational pull on earth is twice that of the sun's and is what creates tides in the ocean as well as what is called an "earth tide," which pulls the crust of the earth toward itself. It's thought that the gravitational pull of the moon and the tides it creates can affect everything from the weather to your mental, emotional, and physical state. Reading that, isn't it an interesting coincidence that in the creation of werewolf stories, the full moon is what triggers their transformations?!

When it comes to using the beautiful, sacred energy of the moon to charge your crystals, you can use the exact same steps as outlined for the sun bath. The only difference is that you will be placing your crystals in direct moonlight as opposed to sunlight. For the best surge of energy, try to time your recharge sessions around the cycles of the new moon or the full moon. I did this during the epic red moon that appeared awhile back and my crystals were buzzing with extra energy.

If time and space allow, a full 24-hour recharge of both sunlight and moonlight could be very powerful for your crystals' energy. For those who are located in more urban areas where tall buildings abound, it is very important that your crystals are placed in direct moonlight or sunlight, so rooftops, balconies, fire escapes, or windowsills are ideal locations.

USING MANTRAS AND AFFIRMATIONS

Repeating mantras and affirmations in conjunction with your crystal healing routine can be a blissfully potent way to connect with your deepest desires. As with programming your crystals with intention, using crystals during meditation or as you chant a mantra or affirmation can help them grow the energy you are looking to invite into your life at a very fast rate. Saying a mantra or affirmation while holding your crystal further projects your desires into the universe and helps them manifest.

A mantra is a word, sound, or phrase that is repeated either silently or out loud that can do one of two things:

1. It can be used as a concentration tool during meditation.
2. It can serve as a personal creed or slogan in your life.

In primordial sound meditation, the type of meditation I teach, the mantras we use are in Sanskrit and are used for their vibrational power (from the sounds they make within your body) and not their literal meanings. Using a mantra this way has the effect of deepening your ability to get centered and release thoughts during meditation.

An affirmation, usually a positive sentence or saying, can be a powerful tool for self-improvement because it rewires the way we think. Affirmations provide encouragement and affirm the beliefs that we want to become true about ourselves and the world we live in. Here are some tips for mantras and affirmations:

* **Act as if the statement is already happening.** It's important to say a mantra or affirmation in the present tense and not as if it's off in the future somewhere. For instance, use "I am..." as opposed to "I will be..." or "I want to..." to create your reality in this moment as your present self.
* **Keep them short and powerful.** These statements don't need to have flowery language or sound like a guru wrote them. Something as simple as "I am successful," or "I deserve love," is a great start.
* **Repeat them as often as you want.** You can say your mantra/affirmation as many times as you like or just once. I've even known people to say them rhythmically like a chant. It can be very powerful to start your day with your saying and/or use it as you are meditating with your crystals.

As you can tell, mantras and affirmations are closely related. For the remainder of this book I will refer to both as mantras. Starting in Chapter 3, I will provide you with a mantra that can be used with each of the crystals you learn about.

3.

Five Crystals to Begin Your Collection

By this point you should have a clear understanding of the history of crystals, how they work, why they work, and how to care for them. Now it's time to choose the right ones for your needs and begin the process of building your collection to transform your life! Starting your collection is such a fun experience. One of my favorite things to do is go on crystal "hunts" when I travel to new cities and countries: finding little shops to walk into or even taking the adventure up a notch and going to the mines themselves! I love picking up crystals with my bare hands to feel their energy and getting pulled in by their colors as I gaze at their facets intently. It's almost meditative how you can get lost while staring at their beauty.

Clear quartz is a mainstay in my ever-rotating crystal collection because of its powerful ability to purify energy, and my very first stone, citrine, was just the tool I needed as I walked into a more evolved version of myself and is something that I am rarely without in my day-to-day life. In this chapter, I will show you how to press start on this healing journey and dive into five crystals that I believe no person should be without. Happy hunting!

CONSIDER WHAT FINISH YOU LIKE

Crystals come in a variety of sizes, colors, and finishes. Before you start your search, you should consider what type of crystals you are most attracted to. You can find crystals that are:

* **Raw and Natural:** Exactly as they came out of the earth.
* **Polished:** Can be smoothed to shine with or without edges on all or one side. This method is typically used to keep parts of the stone in its naturally raw state while smoothing and polishing some areas to highlight its beauty or to make crystals symmetrical or fully rounded.
* **Tumbled:** Placed in a tumbler with other stones until their edges are smooth and they have a polished look all over. This method is usually only done with tiny, small, and some medium-size crystals. (Think of a small concrete mixer filled with crystals.)
* **Cut:** Typically requires a lapidary (stone artist) who uses tools to shape raw crystals into decorative items or jewelry.
* **Gem Quality:** Crystals that fit in this category are of a jewelry quality.

The look of the crystal has no effect whatsoever on the amount of energy or power it will have. You can choose the crystal that looks the best to you. Size, however, *does* matter and the bigger the crystal, the more intense its vibrational frequency. For this reason, it is important to be clear about what you want to do with the crystal before you purchase one. Will it be used for jewelry? As décor in your home or office? Or will it be one that needs to be small enough that you can carry it in your pocket or purse? For me, keeping smaller crystals on my person and larger ones displayed in my home has given me a good balance of energy. All crystals, no matter the size, contain powerful energy, but if you are looking to experience a more intense energy, a larger crystal may be just what you need. Sometimes you just have to go big or go home!

HOW TO CHOOSE THE RIGHT CRYSTAL

Once you decide on the type and size you're after, allow yourself to surrender to the moment and go with your gut, especially if this is your first time choosing a crystal. You may walk into the situation thinking you know what you'll choose or having a certain color preference, but the truth is, when you let your intuition lead you, you will be sure to get the stone that you actually need. As the saying goes, "You don't choose the crystal, the crystal chooses you."

When you first start your crystal journey, you should buy in person whenever possible. Otherwise, purchase crystals from an online seller who provides a good amount of information about each one. When you go into a place that sells crystals, scan the shelves slowly and glide your eyes past each one. You will notice that you are pulled toward specific stones. When you notice a pull (usually it manifests as a desire to touch and hold it), pick it up and hold it in your hands. If there are a few of the same kind that interest you, put them in your hand and close your fingers around them. When you close your eyes and focus on your breathing, you will start to notice that one of the crystals begins to stand out more than others. Once you read up on the particular stone that "chose" you, you'll usually realize its healing properties are a perfect fit.

On the flip side of this, pay close attention to the crystals you come across that seem to repel you as well. Those stones may speak to deeply rooted issues you are avoiding. I'd recommend you pick those up, too, and try to stay open to their use in your life.

If choosing a crystal for a friend or family member, set the intention of finding the right stone for that specific person. Think about who they are and what energy they may need, and then follow the same steps outlined above. Remember, all stones have healing properties so do not overthink this process too much. There are no wrong choices when it comes to crystal selection. Have fun with it!

THE BEST CRYSTALS TO START A COLLECTION

With the thousands of crystals in existence (and new ones popping up regularly), figuring out where to start walking into the world of crystal healing can be, well, overwhelming.

My crystal collection is now in the hundreds, but out of all the stones I have amassed over the years, I find that I keep coming back to these five. I chose to feature these five crystals because of their strong energy and ability to work in multiple facets of your life at once. From home to work and from your past to your present (and even your future), these crystals will not only begin to cause major shifts in your life, but they will also work amazingly well with other crystals you add to your collection. Plus, these are all relatively easy to find at any price point!

CITRINE
for Confidence

Citrine, also known as the "stone of success," is a powerful tool for divine manifestation. Its honey-yellow color brings with it a feeling of warmth and optimism.

DESCRIPTION   Bright honey to deep burnt orange.

WHERE TO USE IT   Keep it at work or wear it as jewelry on important occasions. Place citrine in your safe, cash box, or wallet for added wealth and prosperity. Citrine can be helpful to those experiencing nightmares or insomnia if placed under the bed or your pillow.

WHERE IT'S FOUND   Many crystals being sold as citrine are actually heat-treated amethyst, which is often found in Brazil. It is extremely difficult to tell the difference, but a heat-treated citrine usually has a concentration of yellow/orange at its tips. Natural citrine, which has become more of a rarity, is mined in Spain, France, Russia, Madagascar, and the Democratic Republic of the Congo. Though there is much debate in the crystal community about working with heat-treated citrine, I have found that it still contains a very powerful energy. Its molecular structure is that of amethyst, but because it was transformed, in some ways it resonates with the color energy of yellow/orange (not purple).

SPIRITUAL GROWTH POWERS   Manifestation, confidence, creativity, power. Wearing citrine provides a major confidence boost and feelings of expanded self-esteem. Meditating with citrine will help you unlock deeper layers of yourself so you can move toward a more successful personal path.

PHYSICAL HEALING POWERS Citrine is a good tool for detoxing your body, particularly when trying to break addictive habits and patterns. It can help to relieve anger, depression, and mood swings through its ability to boost confidence and outlook. This crystal stimulates circulation in your body, helps to regulate your metabolism, and aids in your digestion.

CHAKRA Solar plexus. Activate this chakra by wearing a long pendant that will rest between your ribcage and navel or gently place citrine against your skin in that area for deeper healing.

PURPOSE AND FUNCTION

Citrine can help connect you with your life's purpose by guiding you toward new opportunities and empowering you to stay open (mentally and emotionally) in times of difficulty. Citrine also provides great confidence and reminds you of the power in your personal will. This stone is useful for personal and professional goals. When using citrine, be prepared to shed the version of yourself that you have outgrown. At various moments in our lives we experience a certain type of restlessness or frustration that lets us know it's time to level up. Much like when clothes get too small, the skin we are in starts to feel a size too small. Citrine helps point you toward the more evolved version of yourself.

At the beginning of this book, I shared that the first crystal in my collection was a beautiful piece of citrine, and, to this day, I do not leave home without it. It has proven to be a great aid to me when I am going through times of transition or need a boost of confidence in meetings for work.

MANTRA

I am confidently growing into my purpose.

Repeating this with your citrine crystal in hand speaks to
its vibrational ability to lead you toward self-evolution
and boost your confidence during transition.

CLEAR QUARTZ
for Balance

Clear quartz, sometimes referred to as the universal stone, is a must-have for every collection.

DESCRIPTION Colorless. Can also be cloudy or clear and glasslike.

WHERE TO USE IT Can be used anywhere and everywhere. Keep it prominently displayed on your desk or in your office for stimulating clear thinking, focus, and clarity while working. Since clear quartz is a purifier of energy, it can be beneficial to place it in high-traffic areas of the home, like your entryway or living room.

WHERE IT'S FOUND Clear quartz is one of the most abundant healing crystals on earth. It is found all over the world, with each location providing its own unique added energy to its healing properties. Tibetan clear quartz, for example, is thought to be a stone that is powerfully tied to spiritual wisdom, and it has been used to establish contact with the sacred wisdom of ancient cultures. Most often though, commercially used clear quartz is mined in Brazil, Madagascar, and Arkansas.

SPIRITUAL GROWTH POWERS Clarity, balance, cleansing. Meditating with clear quartz can help you access higher realms of spirituality because of its ability to clear energy pathways. It opens up the spirit to higher guidance. This is a very easy crystal to program with intentions. It resonates with your deepest desires.

PHYSICAL HEALING POWERS   Clear quartz is very stimulating to the body, especially the nervous system. It supports hair and fingernail growth and is thought to be a "master healer" stone, as it is useful for healing all types of ailments. In addition, it can help soothe pain from injury, burns, and severe headaches/migraines.

CHAKRA   All. Connected to the root, sacral, solar plexus, heart, throat, third eye, and crown chakras. Place a clear quartz in bathwater or use in a drinking elixir to activate its energy. See Chapter 13 for an elixir recipe.

PURPOSE AND FUNCTION

One of the easiest crystals to find, clear quartz helps balance energy, enhance focus, and bring clarity to its user. This is an amplifier stone, which means that it will amplify any energy or intention that it is around and connects with. For this reason, it is great to use in conjunction with other stones in your collection and a wonderful meditation tool. Though clear quartz does not store negative energy, because it is an amplifier crystal and a powerful conduit of energy, it is important that you charge and cleanse it regularly. I keep pieces of this on hand and sprinkled throughout many of the rooms of my home.

MANTRA

I share my light with others and
I attract their light in return.

Repeating this with your clear quartz crystal in hand
helps you access its vibrational ability to purify energy
and amplify nearby energy for your best good.

GREEN AVENTURINE

for Adventure

Green aventurine, often known as the stone of luck, brings lightness, optimism, and courage into your life.

DESCRIPTION   Ranges from a cloudy seafoam green to bright apple green. This crystal often has iridescent, metallic-colored inclusions made up of other minerals and usually has a sparkly quality to its appearance.

WHERE TO USE IT   Excellent stone to wear as jewelry or to keep in areas where spontaneous good luck is needed. For example, keep a tumbled piece of aventurine in your car for good luck when looking for parking or trying to avoid traffic. With its ability to dissolve anger and stress, this crystal is good for use in the home where a lighthearted energy is needed, like the family room.

WHERE IT'S FOUND   Aventurine is often found in Russia, Brazil, and India. A member of the quartz family, this crystal also comes in blue, brown, and peach hues (each has its own healing properties).

SPIRITUAL GROWTH POWERS   Courage, detachment from outcomes, good luck. Green aventurine is considered to be a crystal of opportunity in both life and love. Using aventurine can help you heal from a painful heartbreak and feelings of disappointment by instilling an understanding that your relationship experiences can still be valuable even if they were only meant to be temporary.

PHYSICAL HEALING POWERS   Green aventurine is beneficial for physical healing of the heart and the eyes. Specifically, nearsightedness, farsightedness, astigmatism, cardiac issues, and circulatory problems. It has also been known to accelerate the growth of underdeveloped infants and children; help fertility problems; and ease eruptions of acne, eczema, and rosacea.

CHAKRA   Heart. Wearing aventurine as a pendant that rests on your heart activates its abilities to heal emotional and physical heart ailments. Best worn against your flesh as opposed to over your clothes.

PURPOSE AND FUNCTION

Green aventurine encourages feelings of vitality and a certain zest for living. It's an excellent stone for navigating obstacles as it helps you see them as opportunities for personal growth. I've noticed that when I carry green aventurine, I encounter a lot of spontaneous luck, like finding good parking spots and coins on the street.

MANTRA

I encounter the best possible outcomes
in all situations I face.

Repeating this with your aventurine crystal in
hand taps into its vibrational ability to bring you
an attitude of acceptance and optimism.

BLACK TOURMALINE
for Protection

Black tourmaline, also called "schorl," is a powerful tool for protecting you from negative or destructive people, as well as dark energy and entities.

DESCRIPTION   Deep black and often rectangular in shape.

WHERE TO USE IT   Place by your front door at home and work. Because this stone is an excellent repellent for negative energy and psychic attacks (which can be as simple as ill thoughts from those who do not wish you well), it's best to keep black tourmaline with you as you travel and when you are around large crowds of people, like at shopping malls, speaking engagements, and events. Also keep it near when you find yourself experiencing challenging environments or circumstances.

WHERE IT'S FOUND   A very abundant member of the tourmaline family, black tourmaline can be found in Maine, California, Sri Lanka, Brazil, Africa, and Afghanistan.

SPIRITUAL GROWTH POWERS   Protection, grounding, detoxifying. black tourmaline helps clear out negative thoughts and storylines we may repeat to ourselves, which allows space for a consistent positive attitude toward life. Because of its grounding qualities, meditation with this crystal will help you release harmful behavior and create a path for more light to enter your life.

PHYSICAL HEALING POWERS Black tourmaline is an excellent purifier and creates a protective barrier against electromagnetic smog and radiation. It also helps remove heavy metal toxins and pollutants from your body. In addition to purifying and detoxing the body, this crystal is also great at removing its waste, especially if you are suffering from constipation or ailments of the colon.

CHAKRA Root. Because of its ability to keep you grounded, having this stone near you activates your root chakra. Holding it in your hands while doing energy healing helps to lengthen and strengthen your root chakra.

PURPOSE AND FUNCTION

Black tourmaline can be very beneficial as a tool for grounding yourself and purifying the energy around you. This crystal is especially helpful to those who spend time in lots of public spaces, in the public eye, or high-traffic work environments because it helps protect you from absorbing other people's energy, specifically those who may not wish you well. This is a crystal that I often share with friends as a gift.

MANTRA

I am fully protected and unmoved by any negative energy that is aimed at me.

Repeating this with your black tourmaline crystal in hand helps protect you and repel negativity.

LAPIS LAZULI

for Inner Vision

Lapis lazuli, a favorite of royals in ancient Egypt, is a stone that will lead you toward inner peace.

DESCRIPTION   A beautiful intense cobalt blue, often found with golden flecks of color throughout.

WHERE TO USE IT   Keep this crystal at home, preferably in the areas where you meditate and the living room.

WHERE IT'S FOUND   Excavated from burial sites in ancient Egypt dating as far back as 4000 B.C., today lapis lazuli is commonly found in the United States, Argentina, Afghanistan, Italy, Russia, and Pakistan.

SPIRITUAL GROWTH POWERS   Wisdom, spiritual growth, compassion, spiritual journeying. Meditation with this crystal can make you better able to access higher states of consciousness and inner peace. Lapis lazuli instills you with a seeker's attitude, which often leads to unlocking psychic abilities, investigating past lives, and heightened intuition. This stone can be really helpful for those working in the fields of journalism and psychology because of its investigative energy and desire to lead you toward wise decisions and universal truths.

PHYSICAL HEALING POWERS   Lapis lazuli can help enhance memory and mental stamina. It also aids those suffering from bruising, menstrual cramping, migraines, and attention-deficit disorder. For an eye infection, rub the affected area with lapis lazuli that has been heated in warm water. For insect bites and inflammation, apply the crystal directly to the area after it has been heated in sunlight.

CHAKRA   Throat, third eye, crown. Hold the lapis lazuli in your hand and touch it to these chakras, encouraging an acceptance of your innate truth.

PURPOSE AND FUNCTION

This stone is all about deep spiritual growth, standing in one's truth, integrity, and compassionate leadership. Lapis lazuli is also a wonderful tool for growing the relationships in your life, as it encourages truthful communication and understanding. Working with this crystal enhances your intuition and encourages you to delve deeply into your innermost emotions and thoughts. Using lapis lazuli will help you access your inner vision—that is, your divinely wise knowledge of self and your place in your relationships and the world. I love keeping this crystal near when I am journaling and meditating because of its connection to the third eye.

MANTRA

In all moments, I choose to stand in my truth and act as my highest self.

Repeating this with your lapis lazuli crystal in hand will promote truthful communication and spiritual enlightenment.

Part Two

CRYSTALS FOR SPECIFIC USES

Though all crystals you encounter can be used for your general good, some are better to use than others for specific purposes in your life. In Chapter 1, I explained that each type of crystal has its own unique particle and energy makeup. To take that understanding even further, each type of crystal also has its own unique beneficial properties. So just like you go to certain stores for specific items or ask certain people for different types of advice, so, too, can you utilize certain crystals to connect with particular areas of the mind, body, and soul. In the next few chapters, I will highlight healing crystals that you can work with to create abundance in the fields of career and purpose, creativity, home, relationships, self-love, physical health, mental health, and spiritual growth.

4.

Crystals for Career and Purpose

The pressure to know exactly what we want and who we will be starts early. By kindergarten, we are faced with the big question: "What do you want to be when you grow up?" The societal pressures to earn, do, and be never seem to take personal evolution or passion into account. Nor are we provided with a road map. "Find your purpose," is a phrase we are starting to hear a lot from motivational speakers and *Instagram* posts alike, but it can be very intimidating to think about.

Stones like amazonite for harmony and malachite for leadership might be just what you need to take yourself to the next level. Working with healing crystals in the realm of career and purpose can lead you to destined opportunities and a deeper level of connection to your inner passions so that you can impact the world in a greater way. In this chapter, you will learn about five healing crystals that should find a permanent home on your desk or in your office. It's time to take control of where you're going!

LABRADORITE

for Creating Magic

Considered to be the "stone of magic," labradorite is a useful conduit for connecting to your greatest destiny and purpose by unlocking hidden potential and sharpening your intuition.

DESCRIPTION   Multicolored and iridescent blend of blue, green, orange, and yellow.

WHERE TO USE IT   Keep on or near you at all times, either by wearing as jewelry or as a small stone carried in your pocket or in your purse. Because this is one of the most universally powerful crystals available, it would be advantageous to pick up several and display them in various rooms of your home and/or workplace—especially the office, living room, and bedroom so you can be near its energy as often as possible.

WHERE IT'S FOUND   Occasionally referred to as "black moonstone" or "spectrolite," this rainbow-colored stone is commonly found in Canada, Mexico, and Russia.

SPIRITUAL GROWTH POWERS   Transformation, strength, intellect, protection. Meditating with this stone allows for a greater flow of energy to happen between your aura and your chakras. A highly protective stone, labradorite also grants access to higher levels of consciousness with ease. It's often used for ritual and magic work.

PHYSICAL HEALING POWERS   A very intuitive stone, labradorite can help uncover illnesses that have unknown causes. It's also known to be an aid for digestion and issues of the colon, as well as the eyes.

CHAKRA   All. Hold it in your hand with your eyes closed and practice slow, focused breathing to activate each chakra.

PURPOSE AND FUNCTION

When working with labradorite, you can awaken to new levels of self-awareness and enlightenment, which can be a powerful agent of advancement in your work life. This crystal is also good for reducing stress and boosting mental stamina and intellect, as well as dispelling negative self-talk and overcoming insecurity. Because it is highly protective, working with this crystal helps you preserve your own energy and blocks people from being able to drain you. Universally, this is a stone that promotes magic and opportunity in your life.

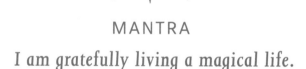

MANTRA

I am gratefully living a magical life.

Repeating this with your labradorite crystal in hand will lead you toward your destiny through opportunities and experiences.

MOOKAITE

for Realizing Your Full Potential

A part of the jasper family, mookaite can aid you in realizing your full potential and enhancing your intuition.

DESCRIPTION   Multicolored, vibrant blend of cream, purple, orange, yellow, and red.

WHERE TO USE IT   Display prominently in your work area and home office for enhanced creativity. Place in a nursery or children's room for a deep child-parent connection and under your pillow for dream recall.

WHERE IT'S FOUND   This fiery earthy stone is named after Mooka Creek in Australia, where it was first discovered. Mookaite is exclusively found in Australia.

SPIRITUAL GROWTH POWERS   Youthfulness, instinct, clarity. Mookaite brings grounding energy and nature into your life. It's also a powerful tool for meditation and dream recall. Meditate with this crystal to ease fears and build self-esteem.

PHYSICAL HEALING POWERS   Mookaite can be a helpful tool during and after pregnancy. Members of the jasper family are known to be regenerative healing stones, especially for muscles, tendons, and blood. This crystal can also be a great help when trying to lose weight, as it speeds up metabolism and counteracts water retention.

CHAKRA   Root and third eye. Meditation with this stone and practicing breathing exercises while seated on the ground help activate these chakras.

PURPOSE AND FUNCTION

This crystal helps cultivate a mentality of agelessness and youthful energy. Good for a motivational boost in the workplace and stimulating the flow of ideas, mookaite also emanates the primal energy of animal instinct and can be used to amplify your own instincts for clear decision-making. A highly intuitive stone, it is also suggested for expectant parents as a way to establish a close connection with their unborn child. Mookaite is as vibrant in appearance as it is filled with intense energy, and it is a great stimulant for creativity and focused action. I enjoy this stone most in its rough and natural form because of its deep connection to nature and grounding properties. It makes for an excellent display piece and jewelry accent!

MANTRA

I am clear in who I am and where I am going.

Repeating this with your mookaite crystal in hand will give you direction and help you create clear plans.

AMAZONITE

for Harmony with Others

Amazonite is considered to be the stone of truth and harmony.

DESCRIPTION Ranges in color from cool teal green to deep cream and khaki brown.

WHERE TO USE IT Anywhere in your office, as well as in your dining or living room. This stone is useful in areas where communication and confrontation happen. Wear a long strand of amazonite beads to give you a surge of courage when confronting inconvenient truths.

WHERE IT'S FOUND Amazonite is sometimes called "Amazon jade" or "Amazon stone" because of large deposits reportedly found long ago in Brazil's Amazon River. This crystal is also found in Russia, India, and the United States.

SPIRITUAL GROWTH POWERS Harmony, peace, boundaries. It helps tremendously with bringing calm to an overactive and overly critical mind. As the "stone of truth," amazonite helps you look for the deepest truth in every encounter. By enhancing your ability to attentively listen to all sides of an issue and find resolve without judgment, this crystal teaches you how to be a creator of inner and outer peace.

PHYSICAL HEALING POWERS This crystal is a great facilitator of general good health. It can aid in cell regeneration and muscle recovery. Rubbing polished amazonite directly on skin issues like blisters, rashes, and acne has been thought to accelerate their healing. It's also considered helpful for childbirth pains.

CHAKRA   Heart and throat. Rub polished amazonite over your throat and heart space to activate these chakras.

PURPOSE AND FUNCTION

Amazonite can encourage you to discover your personal truth, set healthy boundaries, and live with more integrity. This crystal is also helpful for removing fear of confrontation and helping you work out situations with others without judgment. Working with amazonite is useful in the workspace and also with friends and family, so it's good to keep a small piece with you! I have noticed that men especially gravitate to this soothing stone because of its ability to help them vocalize their true feelings. Working with this crystal also lends itself to creativity and problem solving.

MANTRA

I am an honest and thoughtful communicator.

Repeating this with your amazonite crystal in hand
will guide you into the role of mediator.

MALACHITE
for Confident Leadership

Malachite is a good crystal for those looking to become decisive leaders and build more confidence.

DESCRIPTION   A striking, banded swirl of bright and dark greens.

WHERE TO USE IT   Wear malachite as a pendant that lays directly on top of your heart or use it as a display piece on top of your desk to attract confidence and harmony. Because this stone is also an excellent tool for absorbing negativity, it is important to cleanse it often and recharge it in direct sunlight. It is also important to make note that the dust from raw malachite is very toxic if inhaled. I recommend only purchasing polished malachite for your collection.

WHERE IT'S FOUND   Though it's one of the more expensive stones to introduce into your collection, malachite is actually quite common and can be found in Zambia, Russia, Romania, the Middle East, the United States, and the Democratic Republic of the Congo.

SPIRITUAL GROWTH POWERS   Confidence, leadership, protection. Using this stone eases feelings of anxiety, depression, mania, and any fear you may harbor about being yourself. Meditate with this crystal for a dose of positivity and interconnectedness.

PHYSICAL HEALING POWERS Malachite is a helpful tool for joint and muscle pain and can help reduce any swelling or inflammation just by keeping the stone near you. If used in a Reiki healing session, it might be placed on your body.

CHAKRA Solar plexus and heart. Place malachite directly on your solar plexus to absorb any negative emotions and on top of your heart space to bring a feeling of balance and activate that chakra.

PURPOSE AND FUNCTION

Malachite can be especially useful for those with a shy disposition, because it connects you with your inner power and removes the fear of receiving too much attention. This crystal creates a protective barrier against negativity and encourages empathy and understanding toward others, which proves extremely useful for those in a leadership position. It's great for decision-making and motivation, as well as clearing out feelings of confusion. Malachite is an especially beautiful stone in its polished form and makes for a great mala wrap.

MANTRA

I am a leader through my service to others.

Repeating this with your malachite crystal in hand
will encourage empathetic leadership.

CITRINE

for Enhancing Your Personal Power

Citrine is a stone of abundance that will help you find your flow and take your place in the world.

DESCRIPTION   Bright honey to deep burnt orange.

WHERE TO USE IT   Keep at work and wear as jewelry on important occasions. Place citrine in your safe, cash box, or wallet for added wealth and prosperity. Citrine can be helpful to those experiencing nightmares or insomnia if placed under the bed or your pillow.

WHERE IT'S FOUND   Many crystals being sold as citrine are actually heat-treated amethyst, which is often found in Brazil. Natural citrine, which has become more of a rarity, is mined in Spain, France, Russia, Madagascar, and the Democratic Republic of the Congo.

SPIRITUAL GROWTH POWERS   Personal power, manifestation, optimism. Wearing citrine provides a major confidence boost and feelings of expanded self-esteem. Meditating with citrine will help you unlock deeper layers of yourself so you can move toward a more successful personal path.

PHYSICAL HEALING POWERS   Citrine is a good tool for detoxing your body. It's often used when trying to break addictive habits and patterns and can help relieve anger, depression, and mood swings through its ability to boost confidence and outlook. This crystal stimulates circulation in your body, helps to regulate your metabolism, and aids in your digestion.

CHAKRA Solar plexus. Activate this chakra by wearing a long pendant that will rest between your ribcage and navel or gently place against your skin in that area for deeper healing.

PURPOSE AND FUNCTION

Often referred to as the "stone of success," manifestation is the calling card of this yellow beauty. This crystal gives you a positive outlook regardless of the situation so you can maintain a constant level of peace even when under fire. Citrine provides a constant reminder of the personal power each of us holds as it pushes you toward experiences that will lead you deeper into your purpose. Working with this stone can be helpful for growing the relationships in your life and enhancing your awareness of the important roles you play.

MANTRA

I have the power to manifest my destiny.

Repeating this with your citrine crystal in hand
will lead you to success and opportunity.

5.

Crystals for Creativity

Living a fulfilled life and living an inspired live go hand in hand. Creativity is the pulse of your purpose. When you are accessing the creativity you hold within, you are changing the course of history and starting a ripple effect that will impact generations to come. Being able to use your imagination to birth original ideas that are new and valuable is the only way to advance both yourself and the world. Creativity is more than just the production of work stemming from original ideas, it is also part of what shapes your individuality and, ultimately, your reality.

Beautiful stones like red garnet and tiger's eye can help your ideas stand out to powerful people and aid you in finding solutions to difficult problems. Whether you are diving into a new business, looking to spice up your personal life, or trying to start a new chapter in your story, the crystals in this section will make excellent tools for unlocking and enhancing your creative energies. Let's start creating!

RED GARNET
for Enhanced Charisma

A powerful tool for attraction, red garnet carries a magnetic energy that pulls people, opportunity, and creative ideas to its user.

DESCRIPTION   Varies from dark orange-red to burgundy or wine in color.

WHERE TO USE IT   Keep red garnet with you during all important meetings or speaking engagements and put it on display on the nightstand of your bedroom. Add a piece of garnet to your wallet or coin purse to help resolve financial issues.

WHERE IT'S FOUND   This beautiful deep-berry-colored stone is most commonly found in India, Brazil, and Afghanistan.

SPIRITUAL GROWTH POWERS   Vitality, creativity, charisma. Red garnet is a beautiful conduit of joy and support. It helps you to feel confidently rooted in who you are and in the present moment. This is a great stone to have with you in a crisis, as it lends itself to enhancing your instinct to survive. Meditate with this stone to ease anxiety and build self-esteem.

PHYSICAL HEALING POWERS   Garnet is considered to be a very regenerative healing stone. This is a great crystal to work with for issues of the heart, blood, eyes, and lungs. It's also useful for those healing from surgery or wounds. It brings added vitality and energy to your physical life.

CHAKRA Root and heart. Place red garnet directly on these chakra points when you are in a relaxed, meditative state to activate them.

PURPOSE AND FUNCTION

Red or almandine garnet is thought to have come from the Latin word *granatum*, which means "pomegranate." Working with this crystal will enhance your charisma and help others see you in a more attractive and irresistible light. Garnet helps stimulate creativity and transition your ideas from your mind into actionable steps. This stone is a tremendous aid in releasing any panic or anxiety that you may be holding regarding your finances. Also, on the intimacy side of things, it is known to unleash tantric energy for your sex life, revitalize existing energy between lovers, and draw new lovers to you. Red garnet is easily found in small sizes and often seen in the form of cut stones within jewelry (especially men's rings). I enjoy it in its natural geometric shape and often carry it in my Karma Bliss "Bliss Bag."

MANTRA

I attract to my life the opportunities
that will unleash my passion.

Repeating this with your red garnet crystal in hand will
stimulate the passionate energy you hold within.

TANGERINE QUARTZ
for a Curious Outlook

Tangerine quartz is a crystal that is prized for its ability to bring more playfulness and childlike curiosity into one's life.

DESCRIPTION Bohemian rusty orange, often in the shape of a crystal point or in clusters.

WHERE TO USE IT Keep tangerine quartz in your bedroom on your nightstand or under your bed to bring more vigor to your sex life. Utilize it in areas where you find yourself daydreaming often, like the shower or gym.

WHERE IT'S FOUND A member of the vast quartz family, tangerine quartz is most often sourced from Brazil.

SPIRITUAL GROWTH POWERS Curiosity, playfulness, motivation. This crystal is extremely connected to creativity and sexuality. Working with it encourages a hunger for knowledge and wisdom. Meditate with your tangerine quartz crystal to unlock a deeper level of self-awareness.

PHYSICAL HEALING POWERS Tangerine quartz is a great stone to purchase if you have been feeling sluggish or sexually disinterested. This crystal can be very stimulating to your body's glands and can bring lots of vital life force energy to your physical body.

CHAKRA Sacral. Place this crystal directly on your sacral area while breathing deeply with eyes closed to activate this chakra.

PURPOSE AND FUNCTION

Tangerine quartz is said to be very stimulating to your sexual energy and an igniter of creative thought. This stone encourages you to become a motivated seeker of knowledge and ideas. It manifests creativity in your mind as a burst of new ideas and a joyful, adventurous outlook. Working with this crystal helps foster an intense connection between your creativity and your sexuality and can initiate passion throughout all the layers of your life.

This is a fantastic stone to introduce in your work environment, especially if you are a creator (arts, music, writer, graphic designer, photographer, etc.) by trade. It keeps ideas flowing through you at a rapid pace and helps enhance your problem-solving skills when you get stuck. Tangerine quartz looks beautiful as a natural pendant (worn on an extra-long chain or rope) or cluster showpiece for your home.

MANTRA

I honor my life by approaching it with a curious and optimistic outlook.

Repeating this with your tangerine quartz crystal in hand will bring you more insight and exciting experiences.

TIGER'S EYE
for Finding Solutions

Tiger's eye is a great stone for discernment of ideas and opportunities.

DESCRIPTION A banded mix of rich brown and gold sheen. When polished, tiger's eye has an especially luxurious and refined look to it and has been used as protective jewelry for soldiers and as the eyes in statues of gods dating back to the ancient Egyptians.

WHERE TO USE IT Place tiger's eye near the front door to take advantage of its protective qualities and keep it in your office area for help with decision-making and creativity.

WHERE IT'S FOUND Tiger's eye is abundant and found all over the world. Most commonly, though, it is sourced in South Africa, Australia, India, and the United States.

SPIRITUAL GROWTH POWERS Resolution, balance, intuition. Tiger's eye is a highly motivating stone that will help you cultivate a strong intuition and keep an open mind. It's great for helping people break habits of self-destruction and improve decision-making. Meditate with this crystal when in need of discernment.

PHYSICAL HEALING POWERS Tiger's eye is supportive to the digestive system, particularly regarding gas, bowels, and feelings of nausea. It's also useful to enhance vision.

CHAKRA Sacral and solar plexus. Place directly on the navel and two inches below the navel to activate these chakras.

PURPOSE AND FUNCTION

Tiger's eye is used as an amplifier of logic, meaning that it will help you make informed and even-keeled decisions...which is especially useful to curb the sometimes-manic energy that comes along with a highly creative mind. It is also helpful for those who exhibit self-sabotaging behavior and those who tend to purposely create obstacles where there were none. Working with tiger's eye will help clear any creativity blockages. This crystal will add balance to both your emotions and your mind, sharpening your intellect and your intuition. It's a great stone for helping you tune in to those "gut" feelings that can easily be rationalized away and overlooked.

MANTRA

I nurture my creative genius by
balancing my mind and spirit.

Repeating this with your tiger's eye crystal in hand
will promote self-care and reflection.

CARNELIAN

for Taking Bold Action

Carnelian brings a powerful confidence and surge of energy to its user.

DESCRIPTION   Fiery red-orange with a vibrant inner glow.

WHERE TO USE IT   Keep a piece near your work station and also on your person when feeling restless. Carnelian uses its fire energy to bring passion to the spaces it is in. Place it near your front door for protection and as a way to welcome abundance. Keep a small piece with you for accelerated healing when feeling ill. If looking to add passion in the bedroom, keep it near the bed during intimacy—though be careful to remove it from the area before falling asleep, because carnelian's powerful energy can interrupt your sleep.

WHERE IT'S FOUND   Natural carnelian has become more of a rarity on the commercial market. Much of what is sold is actually dyed/heat-treated agate (stripes are a giveaway that it is not natural). The largest amounts of carnelian are found in India. It is also often sourced from Peru, Brazil, and the United States.

SPIRITUAL GROWTH POWERS   Ambition, creativity, courage, boldness. Carnelian is a crystal that helps you manifest your destiny with bold, motivated action. It's helpful for those with a bad temper, and it can bring an energy of balance and tunnel vision–like focus. Meditation with this stone will help you break through limiting thoughts and bring your ideas to fruition. Carnelian can also be used for protection against envy, jealousy, and negative emotions.

PHYSICAL HEALING POWERS   Carnelian helps fight fatigue and laziness by lending a feeling of intense energy and vitality. This is a good stone to use if you have problems with digestion, eating disorders, or poor appetite. Its vibration makes it a great help when experiencing feelings of apathy or depression. Ancient Greeks and Romans often wore this stone as protection against sin, though in modern times we celebrate its ability to encourage willpower and detox the body of alcohol and drugs.

CHAKRA   Root, sacral, and solar plexus. Activate these areas by rubbing a polished piece of carnelian that has been lightly heated with warm water in a circular motion on your chakra points.

PURPOSE AND FUNCTION

Carnelian is a crystal that is especially helpful for those looking to embark on a new career path or wanting to reinvent themselves. Bold action best describes the energy that comes along with working with carnelian. Enhanced ambition, courage in making choices for one's life, as well as bubbling creativity round out many of its energetic uses. This crystal is all about action: getting your body and mind moving with a surge of vital energy so that you can heal yourself on a physical level and accomplish your goals on a mental one. Carnelian can also serve as protection from any envy or jealousy that may be aimed at you.

This is a fantastic stone to keep close when working on projects or making deals. I love having this stone handy when I am creating a vision board for myself and meditate with it often for inner direction on what moves to make.

MANTRA

I take bold action in all areas of my life.

Repeating this with your carnelian crystal in hand will ignite your ambition and fill you with courageous energy.

PYRITE

for Manifestation

Referred to as "fool's gold" since the 1800s because of its golden-brass color, pyrite is actually very valuable as a tool for manifestation.

DESCRIPTION   Golden with a hint of greyish metallic coloring.

WHERE TO USE IT   Use pyrite everywhere. Pair it with other stones to intensify their energies. Place it under your bed or pillow for restful sleep. It's an excellent stone to keep in the areas of your home where you meditate or relax because of its grounding abilities. Keep a piece of pyrite near your home's entrances and windows that have views of other homes to keep noisy or troublesome neighbors at bay.

WHERE IT'S FOUND   Also called "iron pyrite," this metallic healing crystal can be found in the United States, Peru, the United Kingdom, and Spain.

SPIRITUAL GROWTH POWERS   Manifestation, focus, willpower. Working with pyrite can help you overcome fears and grow your confidence. It promotes audacious attitude and encourages you to position yourself in the forefront. Meditate with this crystal to help bring your ideas into reality.

PHYSICAL HEALING POWERS   Pyrite is a great stone to use if you are a restless sleeper or are prone to snoring loudly. It can also help with inflammation and infections. This crystal carries a lot of bold, masculine energy and can be useful for men who are experiencing reproductive issues.

CHAKRA   Solar plexus. Hold in your hands and place a piece of pyrite on your navel while laying down to activate this chakra.

PURPOSE AND FUNCTION

It's no coincidence that pyrite's name shares the same Greek root word (*pyr*) as "pyrotechnics," considering its powerful vibrations are amazing for use in manifesting your dreams. This crystal encourages persistence and commitment toward goals and helps with building an inner resistance to negativity and defeating self-talk. An excellent motivator, pyrite works through your ambition to manifest desire into reality.

This is also a great stone for dynamic leadership and resourcefulness. It can be very helpful to use pyrite while meditating, vision boarding, and building out plans. Hold a piece of pyrite in each hand as you close your eyes and envision your goals coming to fruition. I enjoy these most in their natural nugget form and will usually use one as an enhancement stone, placing it next to another stone that has creative energy for an added boost.

MANTRA

I am committed to the work needed
to turn my dreams into my reality.

Repeating this with your pyrite crystal in hand will enhance your level of willpower to accomplish whatever task is at hand.

6.

Crystals for a Happy Home

Home. Domicile. *Casa*. For most of us, this word, this place, translates on an emotional level as our center and nucleus. Our comforting, protective, and safe space. Your home is a place that should be filled with the energy that brings you closest to your best self. A retreat. Sometimes an escape. An area with an energy that recharges you while it balances and nurtures you. Using healing crystals in your home can have a profound effect on your relationships and on your level of personal happiness. By working with crystals in your home and even featuring them as décor, you are able to change both the dynamic of the energy you are living in and also the experiences you encounter in the world.

Often, home is the place you spend most of your time, so when you thoughtfully place crystals in various rooms around your home, it allows you to soak in their energies for longer periods and boost their effectiveness in your life.

If clutter is an issue in your home (like it sometimes is in mine!), consider using crystals like aquamarine and smoky quartz for more organization and balance. The five crystals that I feature in this chapter will be a great asset to growing joy and happiness in any home environment.

Put away the paint can and close that *Pinterest* tab—it's time to redecorate your space with the vibrations of healing crystals!

SMOKY QUARTZ

for Becoming More Organized

Smoky quartz, sometimes known as the "stone of power," is an incredibly powerful tool for grounding (the practice of becoming rooted to the present moment). It can amplify your ability to be practical and serve as a stabilizing ally during change. Fun fact, in ancient China, smoky quartz was used to make sunglasses!

DESCRIPTION   Varies from a smoky beige and chocolate brown to an opaque grey to black.

WHERE TO USE IT   Keep smoky quartz in the living room or center of the home to encourage organization and simplicity. Keep a small piece near electronics and cell phones to protect against electromagnetic radiation.

WHERE IT'S FOUND   A member of the vast quartz family, this stone is abundantly found in Brazil, Madagascar, Australia, and the United States. The Cairngorm variety, which tends to be more yellow-brown in color, is exclusively found in Scotland and widely used in their jewelry, especially as adornment for kilt pins.

SPIRITUAL GROWTH POWERS Relaxation, organization, grounding. Smoky quartz is a great stress-reliever stone and can be very spiritually grounding. Meditate with this stone to protect your energy and to clear out negativity.

PHYSICAL HEALING POWERS   Smoky quartz is wonderful for relief of headache and menstrual cramp pain. This is a great crystal to use to combat issues related to radiation and protecting against electromagnetic fields. It can also be useful for those experiencing excessive amounts of fluid retention.

CHAKRA   Root. Hold a piece of smoky quartz in each hand and sit quietly with your eyes closed. Practice focused breathing to activate this chakra.

PURPOSE AND FUNCTION

For centuries, smoky quartz has been used as a powerful tool for spiritual and physical grounding to this world, bringing with its use an energy of relaxation, balance, and deep-rooted support. Often used during rituals and ceremonies as a protective shield against emotional and psychic attack, this crystal has even been said to increase your chance of experiencing paranormal phenomena like UFOs, ghosts, and spirit guides.

Smoky quartz is mainly praised for its ability to help you become more practical and organized by curbing materialism and excessive overconsumption. Two years ago, I added a shoebox-sized chunk of smoky quartz (found on a crystal hunt in Austin) to my living room and found myself unable to allow clutter to form anywhere in my home. I now declutter, donate, and toss out belongings about four times per year. This is the perfect crystal to keep close when doing spring cleaning or sorting out finances.

MANTRA

I am prepared for any opportunity because I live in an organized fashion and am grounded to who I am.

Repeating this with your smoky quartz crystal in hand will add a practical angle to the way you see yourself and your world, helping you keep your body and mind both grounded and organized.

RUBY

for Living with Vibrant Passion

Ruby power is unmatched in the crystal world. It carries an energy of fierce passion and exuberant enthusiasm.

DESCRIPTION   Royal, intense red.

WHERE TO USE IT   Keep this crystal wherever you like to start your day for a burst of vital energy and wear it as often as possible as jewelry. Place it under your pillow to ward off nightmares. If there is a display area of your home where trophies, awards, or things that make you feel proud are kept, place a ruby nearby for an increase in your abundance and wealth.

WHERE IT'S FOUND   This highly coveted gem, historically considered to be a stone of royalty, is primarily sourced in India, Thailand, Kenya, Madagascar, and Myanmar.

SPIRITUAL GROWTH POWERS   Passion, prosperity, adventure. Ruby is an extremely high-vibrating stone that uses fire energy to invigorate the body and mind. It encourages a zest for life and can help bring about a more positive mindset. Meditate with this crystal when going through a season of change to focus your mind and cultivate more optimism.

PHYSICAL HEALING POWERS   Rubies are wonderful tools for enhancing your energy. They are also great for aiding issues of the blood; regulating your flow during menstruation; and stimulating the kidneys, adrenal glands, and spleen. Use it when you feel sick for an immune system boost.

CHAKRA   Root. Place a ruby at the base of your spine as you quietly lay down with eyes closed to activate this chakra.

PURPOSE AND FUNCTION

Rubies have long been the favorite of royals, often used more frequently than diamonds because of their invigorating color and powerful properties. This crystal promotes an intense zest for living and is said to stimulate elevated brain activity, abundant wealth, and good health. Ruby can impact your life by giving you a sense of deep personal satisfaction and overwhelming self-acceptance, often manifesting itself as healthy habits and increased metabolism and heightened sensual expression. It lends itself to enhancing your desire for adventure and bringing you the courage to embark on new and uncharted territory. Ruby is a crystal that embodies the phrase "Seize the day!" and can lead to further enjoyment of your daily life.

MANTRA

I live my life courageously and passionately, finding joy in everything I do.

Repeating this with your ruby crystal in hand helps you seek adventure and find fulfillment in your daily life.

AQUAMARINE

for Calming Balance

Aquamarine's energy is just as soothing as its color and helps with calming anger and facilitating clear communication.

DESCRIPTION A Caribbean Sea–like blue-green.

WHERE TO USE IT This crystal can best serve you when placed in areas of the home where there is lots of dialogue and interaction (like the kitchen, living room, and bedroom) because of its ability to defuse hostility and bring an energy of soothing and calm.

WHERE IT'S FOUND Believed by ancient Greeks to be the treasure of mermaids, this sea-blue beauty is found in Brazil, Africa, and the United States.

SPIRITUAL GROWTH POWERS Calming, cooling, refreshing. This is a powerful stone to use when you need to push away negative thinking, as it helps filter out thoughts that are harmful or unwanted. Its legendary calming energy can defuse feelings of fear or phobia. Since the times of the Romans, this crystal has been considered to have the power to ward off forces of evil.

PHYSICAL HEALING POWERS Aquamarine is useful as a detoxifying agent of the organs and as a calming force when experiencing allergies. It can be helpful to wear an aquamarine pendant if you are experiencing thyroid problems, and it can also be beneficial to place pieces of the cool tumbled stone over the eyes if you are having sight issues.

CHAKRA Throat and heart. Place aquamarine on your throat (wearing it as a choker necklace is useful *and* fashionable) and heart space while meditating to activate these chakras.

PURPOSE AND FUNCTION

Coming from the Latin phrase *aqua marina*, which means "seawater," aquamarine brings you an energy of compassion, truthful communication, and personal revelation. You become able to see more deeply into yourself, which allows you to see others through eyes of tolerance and without judgment. The balance aquamarine provides comes from its cooling, gentle energy. Aquamarine is of great benefit to people who have big tempers, helping them defuse anger in trying moments and encouraging them to keep a level head and pragmatic outlook. This stone will help refresh you and relax you into the role of being your highest self.

Though it's closely associated with the words "cool" and "calm," I've found that aquamarine can be intensely empowering through the way it gently helps you express your truth and adapt to the unforeseen flow of life's experiences.

MANTRA

I am calmly certain of my personal power,
and I express my truth with kindness.

Repeating this with your aquamarine crystal in hand will help you calmly navigate any experience you face.

CHRYSOPRASE
for Constant Growth

Chrysoprase is sometimes known as the "stone of the heart." It is a beautiful tool used for forgiveness and finding peaceful closure.

DESCRIPTION A playful apple-green color with a vibrant inner glow.

WHERE TO USE IT Anywhere in your home. It brings balance and optimism to communal areas like the living room and kitchen. Wear it as jewelry (especially a pendant or ring) when seeking spiritual growth.

WHERE IT'S FOUND Many centuries ago, this rare and beautiful stone was sourced primarily in Poland. Today it is commonly found in Australia, South Africa, Brazil, and Russia.

SPIRITUAL GROWTH POWERS Compassion, forgiveness, resolve. Chrysoprase is a powerful tool for forgiveness and for understanding the karmic reasons for the lessons you are experiencing in this life. It can be very useful when looking to heal a broken heart, as it is full of forgiving and compassionate energy. Meditating with this stone will help you see through confusion, ego, and clouded judgment.

PHYSICAL HEALING POWERS Chrysoprase is a great stone for general good health. Using this stone promotes regeneration and youthfulness. It also promotes mental health and helps when experiencing depression. Chrysoprase has been said to help those suffering from schizophrenia.

CHAKRA   Heart. Hold it in your hand with your eyes closed while meditating or wear it as a pendant that falls over your heart space to activate this chakra.

PURPOSE AND FUNCTION

Much like the inner glow it seems to carry when you look at it, chrysoprase has a beautiful ability to help its user go inward to resolve recurring issues and forgive more freely. This crystal has been known to ease depression and anxiety, as well as create a sense of inner peace. It also promotes joy and gentle investigation of suppressed feelings. When using chrysoprase, you will find yourself engaging in lots of self-inquiry about the past and the people you are surrounded by in your life. For this reason, it is an intensely powerful tool for breaking through karmic patterns (the causes behind the choices you repeat or experiences you attract). Chrysoprase is an absolutely wonderful crystal to keep near when seeking out spiritual growth and moving through life lessons.

MANTRA

I walk through life with intuitive compassion and release any energy that binds me to the past.

Repeating this with your chrysoprase crystal in hand will
help you heal unresolved issues and promote the desire
to freely forgive others of any harm you have felt.

WATERMELON TOURMALINE
for a Joyous Attitude

Watermelon tourmaline connects you to a larger understanding of happiness by helping you find joy in all moments, even ones considered to be difficult.

DESCRIPTION   Resembles a sliced watermelon with a pink-red on the inside and green on the outside.

WHERE TO USE IT   Watermelon tourmaline is great as a companion piece carried in your purse, murse (man purse), or pocket. Place it in your bedroom or vanity area to promote self-love and self-care. Use it in the yard or recreation area of your home to encourage adventurousness.

WHERE IT'S FOUND   Made popular in the United States as jewelry in the late 1800s, thanks to Tiffany & Co., this fun and attractive gem is commonly found in Brazil, Africa, Sri Lanka, and the United States.

SPIRITUAL GROWTH POWERS   Happiness, humor, joy. This is a great stone to use when you're feeling down, and it is often referred to as a "feel better" stone. Watermelon tourmaline helps you appreciate the irony and humor in a tough situation and brings balance to your emotions. Meditate with this crystal for greater awareness of self and an increase in joyous feelings.

PHYSICAL HEALING POWERS   Watermelon tourmaline is great for heart health and can improve agility and reflexes. Place it on your forehead to bring centering and calm to your mind.

CHAKRA Heart and the third eye. This crystal is a big activator of the heart chakra when held and meditated with. Placing on or gently rubbing over your forehead can activate the energy of the third eye.

PURPOSE AND FUNCTION

Watermelon tourmaline is a crystal that can support you in every aspect of your journey over your entire life span. Sometimes called the "feel better" stone, this multicolored crystal can help you create a more joy-filled life by leading you to the understanding that happiness is not the result of external experiences. Instead of understanding things with only your brain, you will begin to translate experiences with your heart. Working with watermelon tourmaline will reveal ways you can maintain peace in all moments, even when you are experiencing obstacles or hardship. When you come to this place of awareness, you'll become the lighthearted person who sees the humor in almost everything. This crystal is especially great for drama queens, control freaks, and those who take things too seriously. In moments of sadness or disappointment, I go straight to a piece of this crystal, often carrying it with me for several days as a reminder to "choose happy."

MANTRA

*I am unbounded in my ability to
experience and share happiness.*

Repeating this with your watermelon tourmaline crystal in hand will help you find joy and experience peace in all of life's moments.

7.

Crystals for Love and Relationships

Love and relationships: two of the most complex yet rewarding aspects of our life's journey. Though emotionally, love is often defined as affection, pleasure, or attachment, it mostly manifests itself as a virtue in relation to others. Kindness. Empathy. Understanding. Forgiveness. Sacrifice. Simply put, love itself is an action.

When love is put into action, we are able to form important relationships. The relationships that we have with the people in our lives are in fact meant to be tools for unlocking deeper layers of ourselves. That goes for the blissful and easy relationships as well as the challenging, confusing, and sometimes harmful ones. Relationships with others are not just something we want—they are something we need in order to become who we truly are.

Of course, relationships come in all varieties. Need some extra spice in the bedroom? Shiva lingam has you covered. Want to create a more meaningful friendship? Turquoise can lead you straight to it. In this chapter, we will go over five crystals that can help you enhance and find harmony in the relationships you are currently involved in, as well as attract you to the ones that you need and have not yet found. And yes...this includes crystals that will help you manifest a deeply rooted romantic relationship in your life! Time to bring on the love!

ROSE QUARTZ

for Inviting Romance Into Your Life

Rose quartz, also known as the "stone of love" and the "heart stone," has been used as a tool for nurturing love and relationships since as early as 600 B.C.

DESCRIPTION   Pale pink to a rusty orange-red pink.

WHERE TO USE IT   Should be utilized in all areas of your home. It can be especially powerful for attracting romantic love when placed near the bed on a nightstand or in any other areas of the home that represents marriage or an intimate relationship.

WHERE IT'S FOUND   Another abundant member of the quartz family, rose quartz is somewhat of an oddity in that it is typically only found in large masses, unlike its sibling clear quartz, which is only discovered as small clusters and crystal points. This stone is commonly sourced in India, Brazil, Japan, South Africa, and Madagascar.

SPIRITUAL GROWTH POWERS   Love. Emotional healing. Forgiveness. Romance. Rose quartz is a great stone to use for healing issues of the heart. Meditating with this crystal helps tear down emotional walls that may have been built up because of trauma or negative thoughts and clear out any of that stagnant energy so there is more room for love and intimacy to flow through.

PHYSICAL HEALING POWERS   Rose quartz can be a great addition to your beauty routine because it promotes a youthful appearance and helps to clear and brighten your complexion. It's also good for balancing sex drive and helping with fertility. Rose quartz is known to soothe burns and ease issues of the blood and kidneys. It's ideal for those suffering from heart weakness, imbalance, or trauma.

CHAKRA   Heart. Place rose quartz over your heart with direct skin contact or use as a topical or ingested elixir to activate this chakra. See Chapter 13 for an elixir recipe.

PURPOSE AND FUNCTION

Rose quartz is a powerful tool for major emotional transformation. This crystal helps turn you toward love and ease the pain of any past trauma. It also creates a clear pathway so that you are better able to recognize and receive love from others. Much of its power lies in helping you heal by showing you how to practice forgiveness and how to release memories of hurtful experiences. When you allow yourself to trust again and tear down walls that you have built up against intimacy, you attract the relationships that are meant for you and allow yourself to experience love on a higher level.

Rose quartz can also be helpful in restoring trust in a relationship where betrayal has happened, and encourages unconditional love. I gifted a large chunk of rose quartz to a friend who was coming out of a difficult divorce, and she shared with me that after placing it in her bedroom, she began to feel more optimistic about love, less broken, and began experiencing kindness from people everywhere she went. This attitude of having an openness to life and an acceptance of the painful breakup of her marriage ultimately led her into a new relationship that far surpassed the one she walked away from. I keep a lot of rose quartz on hand and am a big fan of tumbled pieces that come in the shape of a heart.

MANTRA

I keep my heart open so that I may freely give and receive love.

Repeating this with your rose quartz crystal in hand will help you stay open to the possibilities of love and heal from any past emotional pain.

LAPIS LAZULI

for Understanding Karmic Connections

Lapis lazuli, a crystal that has long represented luxury and royal power, is a stone that will lead you to a deeper understanding of your inner truth and karmic ties.

DESCRIPTION A beautiful intense cobalt blue, often found with golden flecks of color throughout.

WHERE TO USE IT Display lapis lazuli stone in areas of your home that you regularly share with your partner. Placing it in the bedroom under your mattress is ideal.

WHERE IT'S FOUND Composed of various minerals, including lazurite and pyrite (where its golden flecks come from), this crystal has been excavated from ancient Egyptian sites as far back as 4000 B.C. Today lapis lazuli is commonly found in the United States, Argentina, Afghanistan, Italy, Russia, and Pakistan.

SPIRITUAL GROWTH POWERS Fidelity, wisdom, spiritual growth, spiritual journeying. This stone can be extremely helpful for those working in the fields of journalism and psychology as well as for those in long-term romantic relationships because of its investigative energy and desire to lead you toward wise decisions and locating universal truths. Working with lapis lazuli in the home can help strengthen romantic relationships and inspire your partner to view you with reverence and compassion.

Meditation with this crystal can lead to an access of higher states of consciousness and deeply rooted inner peace. Lapis lazuli instills you with a seeker's attitude, which often leads to unlocking psychic abilities, investigating past lives, and a heightened intuition.

PHYSICAL HEALING POWERS Lapis lazuli can enhance memory and mental stamina. It also aids those suffering from bruising, menstrual cramping, migraines, and attention-deficit disorder. To help an eye infection, rub the area with lapis lazuli that has been heated in warm water. To soothe insect bites and inflammation, apply the crystal directly to the area after it has been heated in sunlight.

CHAKRA Throat, third eye, crown. Connecting lapis lazuli to these chakras by holding it in your hand encourages self-awareness and acceptance of your innate inner truth. Working with this crystal will help to open your third eye and balance your throat chakra.

PURPOSE AND FUNCTION

Lapis lazuli is a wonderful stone to work with if you are in a long-term romantic relationship because of its ability to facilitate truthful conversation and expose the karmic root of discourse. This stone is all about deep spiritual growth, standing in one's truth, integrity, and compassionate leadership. Lapis lazuli is also known to be a unifying force in relationships and has the power to help couples understand the deeper reasons of why they are present in one another's lives.

It has also been said that lapis lazuli is a stone of fidelity and encourages loyalty and self-reckoning. This is one of the reasons why many people keep a piece of this beautiful stone underneath their bed or mattress. My husband and I both have lapis lazuli bracelets we wear often as a reminder to turn toward one another and communicate in a truthful and thoughtful way. Because of the psychic energy it releases, you just may become one of those in-sync couples (maybe annoyingly so for your friends!) that finishes one another's sentences.

MANTRA

I honor my relationship by behaving as my highest self in all moments.

Repeating this with your lapis lazuli crystal in hand promotes truthful communication and wise decision-making.

TURQUOISE
for Creating Wholeness

Turquoise is considered to be both the stone of friendship and the stone of wholeness. Its energy is known to strengthen emotions and aid in the release of self-limiting behavior.

DESCRIPTION   Blue-green in color, this gem often resembles a nugget and is seen with black/brown veining and inclusions.

WHERE TO USE IT   Keep turquoise in the bedroom and living room for harmony and happiness in your romantic partnerships, and place a piece in your home office or kitchen to attract wealth. This is a great stone to pick up in the form of an amulet and wear when meeting new people.

WHERE IT'S FOUND   Getting its name centuries ago from its popularity in Turkish marketplaces, turquoise is most popular in Iran, New Mexico, and Tibet and is primarily sourced in China, Myanmar, Egypt, Mexico, Peru, France, the Middle East, and the United States.

SPIRITUAL GROWTH POWERS   Spiritual depth, emotional balance, friendship, wholeness. Turquoise helps release feelings of loneliness and isolation and covers you with a confident and open-minded outlook that is useful for building new friendships. When meditating with turquoise, it is typical to experience feelings of peace, well-being, and calm. Turquoise can also be used for protection while traveling and as a communication aid while speaking in public.

PHYSICAL HEALING POWERS   Because of its ability to provide energy of peace and calm, turquoise is often used by those suffering from anxiety, depression, stress, and emotional pain. It is also said to be useful as protection against pollution and as an aid when experiencing inflammation, stomach problems, and allergies.

CHAKRA   Throat. Activate your throat chakra by holding turquoise in your hand with closed eyes and imagining white light flowing from it to you for several moments.

PURPOSE AND FUNCTION

Turquoise teaches wholeness by amplifying your emotional intelligence and pushing its energy through you in the form of kindness and generosity to others. By acting in service to others, you are actually unlocking the desires you have for yourself and clearing a pathway for random acts of reciprocity to reach you. Turquoise helps calm and restructure the thoughts of a person with a negative, skeptical, or suspicious mind, transforming them into more open, accepting, and selfless individuals. This crystal strengthens your connection to the spirit realm and guides you to discovering your true path in life, also helping you release past regrets and appreciate "what is." When all of these attributes begin to come together in your life, it allows for a sense of wholeness to build inside of you.

When you feel whole, you are operating as the best version of yourself and can experience relationships and friendships at their highest level, detached from drama, expectation, or outcomes. I highly recommend this stone for the reserved and shy, as well as those looking to have more impactful interactions with the people in their lives! I'm a big fan of the silver and turquoise bracelets that are often found in Arizona and New Mexico.

MANTRA

I am building a life of wholeness, not perfection.

Repeating this with your turquoise crystal in hand will teach you the art of blissful acceptance and release of stagnant thoughts.

SHATTUCKITE

for Growing Your Intuition

Shattuckite is a stone that can assist you in growing your intuition and enhancing any undiscovered psychic abilities.

DESCRIPTION   A vibrant mix of light blue and deep blue, sometimes with an addition of green throughout.

WHERE TO USE IT   Keep shattuckite in sacred areas of your home or use it in spaces where you like to meditate and/or relax. Since this is a great crystal for those who do a lot of public speaking, it would be useful to find a travel-sized piece that you can carry with you.

WHERE IT'S FOUND   First discovered in Arizona at the Shattuck mine, this crystal is commonly sourced in the United States, Germany, Greece, South Africa, Argentina, the Democratic Republic of the Congo, and Great Britain.

SPIRITUAL GROWTH POWERS   Intuition, psychic ability, integrity. Shattuckite helps open up the spiritual pathways residing within you to connect you to the spirit realm. It represents sacred truth and can aid you in uncovering areas in which you need to improve. Working with this crystal will guide you toward living at a higher vibration. Use it during meditation to awaken your third eye and enhance your psychic ability.

PHYSICAL HEALING POWERS   Shattuckite is thought to be an aid for general good health and is often used in elixirs and tonics. This stone also helps provide balance for acidity in the body and can help with issues of the blood.

CHAKRA Throat and third eye. Because this crystal shares an intense spiritual and sacred energy, it is beneficial to use it as an essence (see Chapter 13 for essence recipes). Once you have steeped this crystal in spring water, activate your chakras by patting the essence on your forehead and throat areas.

PURPOSE AND FUNCTION

Shattuckite represents deep, sacred truth. It helps you better understand the underlying meanings to things and to live a life with more integrity. You know the saying "If you're going to talk the talk, you better walk the walk"? Well, shattuckite helps you do just that by holding space for you to understand that in order to expect change in others, you must be willing to change yourself too. Using this stone for love will teach you the balance that is required for a successful relationship. Shattuckite has been one of my favorite stones to work with over the past year. Since wearing it as a ring, I've noticed that my dreams are a lot more intense and usually give me insight into small things I will experience in the coming days.

MANTRA

I am both a teacher of truth and
a student of the universe.

Repeating this with your shattuckite crystal in hand will lead you toward sacred truth and help you live as the change you wish to see.

THE ENERGY OF

crystals

CAN TRANSFORM YOU

MENTALLY,

PHYSICALLY,

EMOTIONALLY,

AND

SPIRITUALLY

Amazonite

Amazonite is considered to be the stone of truth and harmony. It can lead you to inner peace through self-inquiry.

See pages 70 and 121

Amethyst

Amethyst is a powerful tool for soothing the emotions and has been used for thousands of years as a defense against overindulgence and an aid in overcoming addictions. It also facilitates awareness and protection during spiritual exploration.

See page 157

Angelite

Angelite is a high-vibration stone that can increase your ability to communicate with the angel realm and receive guidance from your spiritual guardians.

See page 161

Aquamarine

Aquamarine's energy is just as soothing as its color and helps with calming anger and facilitating clear communication.

See page 95

Black Obsidian

Also known as "Apache tear," black obsidian is a volcanic glass that helps you face unpleasant truths so you can work through and release them.

See page 165

Black Tourmaline

Black tourmaline, also called "schorl," is a powerful tool for protecting you from negative or destructive people, as well as dark energy and entities.

See page 59

Bloodstone

Also referred to as "heliotrope" or "Christ stone," bloodstone is a useful ally during times of change and is a powerful tool for calming aggression.

See page 149

Blue Lace Agate

Blue lace agate is a great tool for communicating spiritual ideas and calming those who are mentally overstimulated.

See page 151

Carnelian

Carnelian offers a powerful confidence and surge of energy. It is a stone of action and vibrant passion, most often used for accelerated healing and increased vitality.

See pages 84 and 137

Chrysoprase

Chrysoprase is sometimes known as the "stone of the heart." It is a beautiful tool used for forgiveness and finding peaceful closure.

See page 97

Citrine

Citrine, also known as the "stone of success," is a powerful tool for divine manifestation. Its honey-yellow color brings with it a feeling of warmth and optimism. Citrine is a stone of abundance that will help you find your flow and take your place in the world.

See pages 51 and 74

Clear Quartz

Clear quartz, sometimes referred to as the universal stone, is a must-have for every collection.

See page 54

Fluorite

Fluorite is a powerful stone for activating the mind and enhancing focus, as well as good decision-making, by clearing you of confusion and cleansing your chakras.

See page 144

Gold Tektite

Gold tektite is a beautiful stone for uncovering your personal power and strengthening your will.

See page 178

Green Aventurine

Green aventurine, often known as the stone of luck, brings lightness, optimism, and courage into your life.

See page 57

Green Jade

Known as a stone for health and dreams, green jade is believed to be a link between the physical and spirit world that can also restore the body to optimal health.

See page 130

Hematite

Hematite is a powerful tool for strengthening the body and protecting your spiritual life, often used as a conduit for manifesting your desires.

See page 140

Kyanite

Kyanite offers powerful emotional healing through self-examination and intuitive guidance.

See page 163

Labradorite

Considered to be the "stone of magic," labradorite is a useful conduit for connecting to your greatest destiny and purpose by unlocking hidden potential and sharpening your intuition.

See page 66

Lapis Lazuli

Lapis lazuli, a favorite of royals in ancient Egypt, is a stone that will lead you toward inner peace, your inner truth, and your karmic ties.

See pages 61 and 105

Lepidolite

This purple powerhouse can help you push through paralyzing anxiety and bring you enhanced mental abilities.

See page 153

Mahogany Obsidian

Mahogany obsidian is a volcanic glass that helps you confront and work through limiting thoughts so that you may experience more abundance in your life.

See page 126

Malachite

Malachite is a good crystal for those looking to become decisive leaders and build more confidence.

See page 72

Moldavite

Moldavite is a tremendous tool for spiritual activation and transformation.

See page 170

Mookaite

A part of the jasper family, mookaite can aid you in realizing your full potential and enhancing your intuition.

See page 68

Image © Getty Images/Estellez

Moonstone

Moonstone is also known as a stone of feminine mystery and is powerfully tied to fertility and hormonal balance in women.

See page 135

Image © Getty Images/J-Palys

Nuumite

Also known as "the sorcerer's stone," nuumite is a crystal for enhancing your personal magic and manifesting synchronicities.

See page 172

Image © Getty Images/Ron Evans

Pyrite

Referred to as "fool's gold" because of its golden-brass color since the 1800s, pyrite is actually very valuable as a tool for manifestation.

See page 87

Red Garnet

A powerful tool for attraction, red garnet carries a magnetic energy that pulls people, opportunity, and creative ideas to its user.

See page 78

Rhodonite

Rhodonite is a stone of restoration that can lead you to a greater understanding of your self-worth and an enhanced self-esteem.

See page 116

Rose Quartz

Rose quartz, also known as the "stone of love" and the "heart stone," has been used as a tool for nurturing love and relationships since as early as 600 B.C. Rose quartz is also used as a powerful divination tool when seeking guidance in matters of the heart.

See pages 102 and 118

Image © Getty Images/benedek

Ruby

Ruby power is unmatched in the crystal world. It carries an energy of fierce passion and exuberant enthusiasm.

See page 93

Image © Getty Images/ikonacolor

Selenite

Selenite is a powerfully cleansing stone that helps clear blockages and purify energy.

See page 174

Image © Getty Images/VvoeVale

Serpentine

Serpentine is an exceptional tool for awakening vital energy in your body and connecting you to nature on a profound level.

See page 133

Shattuckite

Shattuckite is a stone that can assist you in growing your intuition and enhancing any undiscovered psychic abilities.

See page 111

Shiva Lingam

Shiva lingam is a crystal that can activate "kundalini" energy, leading you to a surge of vitality and spiritual transformation.

See page 113

Shungite

Shungite is an antioxidant powerhouse that is said to have the ability to promote good health.

See page 176

Smoky Quartz

Smoky quartz, sometimes known as the "stone of power," is an incredibly powerful tool for grounding (the practice of becoming rooted to the present moment). It can amplify your ability to be practical and serve as a stabilizing ally during change.

See page 90

Spirit Quartz

Spirit quartz is a powerful tool for facilitating your spiritual evolution so you may live as your highest self.

See page 159

Tangerine Quartz

Tangerine quartz is a crystal that is prized for its ability to bring more playfulness and childlike curiosity into one's life.

See page 80

Tiger's Eye

Tiger's eye is a great stone for discernment of ideas and opportunities.

See page 82

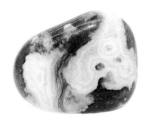

Tree Agate

Tree agate, sometimes known as "dendritic agate," is a powerful tool used for easing mental stress and creating shifts in perspective and ego.

See page 147

Turquoise

Turquoise is considered to be both the stone of friendship and the stone of wholeness. Its energy is known to strengthen emotions and aid in the release of self-limiting behavior.

See page 108

Watermelon Tourmaline

Watermelon tourmaline connects you to a larger understanding of happiness by helping you find joy in all moments, even ones considered to be difficult.

See page 99

Singing Bowl

Using the vibrational, sacred sound of a singing bowl is an incredible way to clear out stagnant or negative energy during crystal cleansing.

See pages 40 and 180

SHIVA LINGAM

for Kundalini Awakening

Shiva lingam is a crystal that can activate "kundalini" energy, leading you to a surge of vitality and spiritual transformation.

DESCRIPTION   Khaki gray with dark brown stripes and swirls. Always in an oval-egg shape.

WHERE TO USE IT   Utilize shiva lingam in the bedroom, displayed on the nightstand, or on a table facing the bed. It provides transformative energy when held during meditation.

WHERE IT'S FOUND   Shiva lingam, also known as "lingam" and "narmadeshvara lingam," is primarily found in India, coming from the Narmada River. They are commonly in the shape of an elongated oval egg, which is said to represent the sacred male energy of the universe.

SPIRITUAL GROWTH POWERS   Sexual energy, kundalini awakening, transformation. Shiva lingam is a very sacred stone for those who practice Hinduism; its name is derived from the Hindu god Shiva. When meditating with this crystal, expect to experience levels of meditation you have not yet reached.

PHYSICAL HEALING POWERS   For centuries, shiva lingam has been worshiped as a tool to create enhanced sexual ability and as a fertility aid. Can also be useful for menopause, impotence, and sexual imbalances.

CHAKRA   All. The power of the shiva lingam stone is capable of charging your entire chakra system. Hold directly against any of your seven chakra points to activate those areas.

PURPOSE AND FUNCTION

Shiva lingam represents inner transformation and kundalini awakening (major shifts in energy and consciousness). This crystal is known to provide you with a surge of vitality that connects to both spiritual and physical energy. Shiva lingam is all about reaching heightened levels mentally, spiritually, and sexually. Over the centuries, it has been thought to hold ancient knowledge of the universe and enlightened consciousness. For that reason, it is often used during sacred rituals and has been an object of worship by different communities over time. This crystal is a great addition to your collection if you are looking to bring more sexual energy to your relationship or if you are trying to boost vital energy and spiritual power in yourself.

MANTRA

I am transforming myself in every moment.

Repeating this with your shiva lingam stone in hand will connect you to your higher self and fill you with vital energy.

8.

Crystals for Self-Love

I am a firm believer that the most important relationship that you can nurture is the relationship that you have with yourself. Often times more dramatic than a soap opera and definitely with more ups and downs than any roller coaster, the relationship YOU have with YOU is like checking the "It's complicated" box on your *Facebook* profile. The road to self-love can be a long and bumpy one. It's not as simple as the sayings we read, like "You need to love yourself!" or "If you don't love you, you can't love anyone else."

Many factors keep us from being able to love ourselves fully: fear, shame, storylines we create in our minds, past experiences, dogma. My friends laugh when I say this, but a piece of raw amethyst saved my life. My life was BIG and fun and full, and yes, I deeply liked a whole lot of things about myself; but an emotional storyline I created in my mind while still a child kept this unrelenting thought of being unworthy firmly cemented in me. When I started working with crystals, I'd often use amethyst when I meditated or felt down for its ability to get through to the underlying issues behind emotional patterns and habits. It helped me break free.

When looking to create more self-love, a few things are very important: protecting yourself, being mindful, practicing forgiveness, living boldly, and engaging in self-care. The five crystals in this chapter will help get you to a place of fearless self-love. So, who's ready to fall in love with themselves?

RHODONITE

for Feelings of Self-Worth

Rhodonite is a stone of restoration that can lead you to a greater understanding of your self-worth and an enhanced self-esteem.

DESCRIPTION   Ranges in color from rose-red to brownish pink. Black veining and splotches are often present.

WHERE TO USE IT   Display rhodonite in the center of your home to balance its energies or drop it into bathwater for a boost of self-love.

WHERE IT'S FOUND   Rhodonite is often found in the United States, Australia, South Africa, Mexico, and Madagascar.

SPIRITUAL GROWTH POWERS   Self-esteem, compassion, balance, love. Rhodonite is wonderful for providing mental balance and calming anxiety. Meditate with this crystal regularly to unlock feelings of unconditional spiritual love for yourself.

PHYSICAL HEALING POWERS   Rhodonite has been known to stimulate circulation, strengthen the heart, encourage bone growth, reduce inflammation in the joints, and ease the pains of arthritis. On a mental level, this crystal has also been prized for its abilities to minimize anxiety and stress.

CHAKRA   Heart chakra. Hold it while meditating or soak in a tub of bathwater that has the essence of rhodonite in it to activate the heart chakra.

PURPOSE AND FUNCTION

Rhodonite provides balance for your yin-yang energies—the Chinese philosophy that describes the interconnectedness of opposite forces (the duality of light and dark and why they are both incredibly necessary in our lives). It's great for connecting you to your inner worth. Working with this stone removes the clouding you may view yourself with to reveal your true value. Once charged with this accelerated self-esteem, you will begin to uncover hidden gifts and talents and move boldly in sharing them with the world.

Rhodonite also encourages understanding, forgiveness, and release of resentment. It helps you to free yourself of the thoughts and feelings that keep you stuck in a state of non-growth. First Lady Michelle Obama's quote "When they go low, we go high" is a perfect embodiment of this stone when it comes to its ability to dissolve any thoughts of revenge or retaliation that you may be harboring. This crystal uses the energy of pure love to help you hug your broken pieces and remember yourself as whole and enough.

Rhodonite is especially useful for those healing from a breakup or who feel that they must always be surrounded by distractions, helping you to find value in enjoying your own company.

MANTRA

I stand in the knowingness that I am worthy of peace and happiness.

Repeating this with your rhodonite crystal in hand will lead you toward greater self-love through understanding your inner value.

ROSE QUARTZ

to Open the Heart

Rose quartz, also known as the stone of love or the "heart stone," is often used as a powerful divination tool when seeking guidance in matters of the heart.

DESCRIPTION   Pale pink to a rusty orange-red pink.

WHERE TO USE IT   Can be displayed in the home or as jewelry. It is especially powerful for opening the heart to turn toward itself, which will build up the amount of love and peace that you feel for yourself. Wear it as jewelry—a pendant that falls over your heart is best—and keep a small tumbled version on you regularly.

WHERE IT'S FOUND   Another abundant member of the quartz family, Rose quartz is somewhat of an oddity in that it is typically only found in large masses, unlike its sibling clear quartz, which is only discovered as small clusters and crystal points. This stone is commonly sourced in India, Brazil, Japan, South Africa, and Madagascar.

SPIRITUAL GROWTH POWERS   Love. Emotional healing. Forgiveness. Romance. Rose quartz is a great stone to use for healing issues of the heart. Meditating with this crystal helps tear down emotional walls that may have been built up because of trauma or negative thoughts and clear out any of that stagnant energy so there is more room for love and intimacy to flow through. It helps you to not only forgive others but to also forgive yourself.

PHYSICAL HEALING POWERS Ancient Egyptians believed that rose quartz could prevent aging. Today it is often used in creams and elixirs for that same reason. Rose quartz can be a great addition to your beauty routine as it lends itself to a youthful appearance and helps clear and brighten your complexion. It's also good for balancing sex drive and helping with fertility, especially if purchased in the form of a medium-sized or small egg. If you're interested in working with rose quartz for deep healing and matters of the reproductive system, I'd recommend you consider using a Yoni Egg; though I must warn you, this method is not for the faint of heart and requires inserting the crystal egg into a woman's most private part.

CHAKRA Heart. Place it over the heart with direct skin contact or use as a topical or ingested elixir to activate this chakra. See Chapter 13 for an elixir recipe.

PURPOSE AND FUNCTION

Rose quartz encourages you to treat yourself with gentleness and thoughtful reflection.

It is a powerful tool for major emotional transformation. This crystal helps turn you toward love and ease the pain of any past trauma. It also creates a clear pathway so that you are better able to recognize and receive love from others and from yourself. Much of its power lies in helping you heal by showing you how to practice forgiveness and how to release memories of hurtful experiences. When you allow yourself to trust again and tear down walls that you have built up against intimacy, you attract the relationships that are meant for you and allow yourself to experience love on a higher level.

This crystal also helps you draw love toward yourself. Rose quartz has the ability to purify and open your heart on all levels, which can result in a deep inner healing. Occasionally I have the bad habit of being overcritical of myself when starting new projects. For this reason, I keep a heart-shaped tumbled piece of rose quartz with me as part of my daily armor when I am working. I've found that doing this has instilled a more accepting and supportive self-talk pattern within me.

MANTRA

In all moments, I will gift myself with unconditional love.

Repeating this with your rose quartz crystal in hand will help you open your heart on all levels.

AMAZONITE

for Self-Examination

Amazonite is considered to be the stone of truth and harmony. It can lead you to inner peace through self-inquiry.

DESCRIPTION   This multicolored stone ranges in color from vibrant teal green to a deep cream and khaki brown.

WHERE TO USE IT   Place this stone anywhere in your office space as well as in your dining or living room. This stone is useful in areas where communication and confrontation are required. Wear a long strand of amazonite beads to give you a surge in courage when confronting inconvenient truths.

WHERE IT'S FOUND   It is sometimes called "Amazon jade" or "Amazon stone" because of large deposits reportedly found long ago in Brazil's Amazon River. This crystal is also found in Russia, India, and the United States.

SPIRITUAL GROWTH POWERS   Harmony, inner peace, boundary setting, communication. As the "stone of truth," amazonite helps you to look for the deepest truth in every encounter. By enhancing your ability to attentively listen to all sides of an issue and find resolve without judgment, this crystal teaches you how to be a creator of inner and outer peace.

PHYSICAL HEALING POWERS   This crystal is a great facilitator of general good health. It can aid in cell regeneration and muscle recovery. Rubbing polished amazonite directly on blisters, rashes, and acne has been thought to accelerate their healing. It's also considered helpful for child-birth pains.

CHAKRA   Heart and throat. Rub polished amazonite over your throat and heart space to activate these chakras.

PURPOSE AND FUNCTION

Amazonite can bring you a deep level of inner understanding. It promotes self-inquiry, believing that investigating the root of your own feelings and belief systems can bring you peace and increase your ability to interact with others in a meaningful way. This crystal encourages you to discover your personal truth, set healthy boundaries, and live with more integrity. It is also helpful for removing fear of confrontation and helps you work out situations with others without judgment. Working with this stone can lead you to experience harmony within yourself and toward inner and outer peace.

Amazonite is also helpful for those who suffer from feelings of loneliness, as well as those who are unsure of their place in the world. When I first launched KarmaBliss.com, we sold a multi-beaded amazonite necklace. One of the most interesting things about having an online store is that you are able to pull up all sorts of analytics on who is buying what, and I noticed that 90 percent of the sales of this piece were transactions made by men. Though this crystal is incredibly useful for anyone and everyone, I've come to notice that it especially resonates with men because of its ability to help them express their feelings and dig deeper into their emotional makeup—which historically is an area most fellas are not encouraged to venture into.

MANTRA

*I create peace in my life by exploring
the root of my thoughts and feelings.*

Repeating this with your amazonite crystal in hand will help guide
you to your highest self through regular self-examination.

AMETHYST

for Releasing Bad Habits

Amethyst is a powerful tool for soothing your mind and emotions and has been used for thousands of years as a defense against overindulgence and an aid in overcoming addictions.

DESCRIPTION   Light violet to deep mauve and can be found in various forms like banded masses, geodes, and gem-quality crystal clusters.

WHERE TO USE IT   Wear amethyst jewelry as protection against addictive behavior and place it in all areas of your home for stability and support.

WHERE IT'S FOUND   One of the most popular gems in the world, amethyst is commonly found in Mexico, Africa, Canada, Russia, and Brazil.

SPIRITUAL GROWTH POWERS   Releasing addictions, overcoming fears, divine communication, wisdom. Meditate with amethyst to unveil the unseen motives and reasons behind your behavior. It provides a calming effect that defends against stress and negative energy, encouraging you to find supportive and stable environments in which to grow.

PHYSICAL HEALING POWERS   Often incorporated in treatments for alcohol and drug addictions, working with amethyst can also help with addictions to food and gambling. In addition, this is a great crystal for strengthening the immune system and bringing balance to the brain and nervous system. Place a piece of amethyst under your pillow to help with insomnia and rub a tumbled or polished piece on your forehead to dissipate headaches.

CHAKRA   Third eye and crown. Hold amethyst in your hand and gaze into it imagining white light radiating from it to activate your chakras.

PURPOSE AND FUNCTION

The name "amethyst" stems from the Greek word *amethystos*, which translates as "not intoxicated." For centuries, this crystal has represented self-control and sobriety. Known to help you overcome addiction, amethyst works its magic by uncovering the deeper-rooted issues that lead to addiction in the first place and aids you in understanding and then releasing them. A friend who is in recovery from addiction recently described his amulet made of the gem as "protection from the things that haunt him."

When using this stone, expect to have many "aha" moments, as it creates a free-flowing pathway between you and the divine energy of the universe. Amethyst surrounds you with a light of protection as it encourages spiritual exploration and self-discovery.

MANTRA

I am in control of my behavior and only choose the paths that serve my highest good.

Repeating this with your amethyst in hand will move you away from addictive behavior and provide a feeling of stability and happiness.

MAHOGANY OBSIDIAN
for an Outlook of Pure Potential

Mahogany obsidian is a volcanic glass that helps you confront and work through limiting thoughts so that you may experience more abundance in your life.

DESCRIPTION   Its hue is a spotted mix of glossy black and reddish brown. It's glasslike in appearance and feel.

WHERE TO USE IT   Use when experiencing emotional hardship by holding it or placing it under your pillow while you sleep. It can also be useful to place a larger piece of this near the front and bedroom doors of your home in order to protect your personal energy and space from any unwelcome energy the people entering these areas could be carrying.

WHERE IT'S FOUND   A member of the vast volcanic rock obsidian family, mahogany obsidian is primarily found in Mexico.

SPIRITUAL GROWTH POWERS   Rebirth, release of past, encouragement, ambition. Mahogany obsidian can give you the strength to stand on your own and release limiting thoughts that have kept you viewing life from a place of lack. Meditation with this crystal reveals opportunities to confront past experiences head-on and courageously slay your dragons. It can help you exchange negative, defeating, or stagnant thoughts for a more positive and ambitious mindset.

PHYSICAL HEALING POWERS   Mahogany obsidian brings with it vitality, helping raise your body's overall energy level. It is also known to strengthen the body's organs and its detoxification process, aiding in digestion and the dissolving of blockages. When placed under your bed or pillow, this stone can help draw out stress and tension.

CHAKRA   Root. Lay down on your stomach with your arms at your sides and a piece of mahogany obsidian placed at the base/root of your spine (your lower back where your tailbone is located). As you meditate, envision the color red radiating in that space to activate this chakra.

PURPOSE AND FUNCTION

Mahogany obsidian helps free you of negative thoughts, patterns, memories of abuse, and fears that originated in this lifetime or are karmically linked to past lifetimes and/or the ancestral generations before you. By operating in the present and the past on your behalf, it allows space for a "phoenix" (rebirth) process to occur in your life. This is a crystal that can help set you free by bringing painful emotions and unpleasant truths to the surface so that you can work through them and come out on the other side healed.

Because of its high vibrations of vital energy, this rock also provides the motivation and inspiration needed for you to achieve your goals. Mahogany obsidian will aid you in moving your mindset from a place of lack and limitation to a place of pure potential and abundance.

MANTRA

I will push past limiting thoughts and embrace the blessings of my life.

Repeating this with your mahogany obsidian rock in hand will cleanse you of limiting beliefs and impart an understanding of your greater place in the universe.

9.

Crystals for Physical Health

Self-love and higher consciousness cannot truly exist until you treat your physical health with as much importance and consideration as your mental and emotional health. Nothing exists by itself alone. Optimal health is an intricate balance of mind, body, and soul. Eastern medicine, specifically in India and China, has been utilizing crystals to accelerate healing since its earliest civilizations. In Ayurveda, it is taught that all disease begins when we are living out of harmony with our environment. Even in Western medicine, it has been proven that any stress we face can be internalized and manifested into major illness. Unfortunately, sometimes we experience devastating health issues that are indeed outside of our control. More commonly though, we are able to prevent poor health from manifesting through creating balanced energies, engaging in mindful repetitive action, and utilizing crystal energy.

Fact is, we each get one chance to love and honor the vessel that we currently inhabit. No matter your current routine, there is always room for improvement. Whether you are facing issues like weight (over or under) and a common cold, or you are walking through ailments that are more severe like chronic pain and disease, throughout history crystals have been used by healers to alleviate symptoms and achieve total healing. Cheers to manifesting a life filled with good health!

GREEN JADE

for Detoxification

Known as a stone for health and dreams, green jade is believed to be a link between the physical and spirit world that can also restore the body to optimal health.

DESCRIPTION Varies in shades of creamy light green, vibrant apple green, and deep forest green. Jade can also come in blue, white, red, lavender, and orange.

WHERE TO USE IT Wildly popular as jewelry, wear a piece of jade as a bracelet or necklace regularly to support a balanced body and mind. Place it against the forehead to recall dreams and display in the family room of your home for good luck.

WHERE IT'S FOUND Jade comes in two forms: jadeite (harder and more valuable) and nephrite (softer and more common). The hardness of a crystal is based on the Mohs scale of mineral hardness, which tests a stone's ability to be scratched, and is not something you will likely be able to sense with a touch of your hand. Telling the difference between jadeite and nephrite can be very difficult for experts and almost impossible for an average person's naked eye. Jadeite can be found in Russia, China, and Guatemala, while nephrite is additionally found in New Zealand and the Swiss Alps.

SPIRITUAL GROWTH POWERS Health. Balance. Nourishment. Protection. Green jade is a stone of new beginnings and opportunities. It can help bring you self-acceptance and harmony in your relationships. Meditate with this stone to calm your mind and remember insightful dreams.

PHYSICAL HEALING POWERS   Green jade heals by helping to detox the body and regenerate tissues. It is also great for the lymphatic system, as well as your skin and hair. Green jade also has been said to be helpful with mental disorders like schizophrenia.

CHAKRA   Heart. Unblock and activate this chakra by wearing jade around your neck or holding it on the skin.

PURPOSE AND FUNCTION

A favorite of Chinese royals, green jade has been found in burial sites dating as far back as the Neolithic period. This is a powerful cleaning stone for the body and is often utilized in spas, saunas, and skin products around the world for its abilities to detox and purify. Green jade is especially supportive in eliminating toxins from the organs and helping issues of the bones, joints, and hips. Using jade will help you integrate the mind and the body.

Though it has been used for beauty over many thousands of years, jade has recently surged in popularity all over social media in the form of face and body rollers. These rollers are very effective at restoring a youthful appearance and flushing out any fluid retention you may be experiencing. I especially love using a jade rolling tool on my face after a long flight or long night to look and feel more rested.

MANTRA

My body regenerates and releases toxins with ease.

Repeating this with your green jade crystal in hand
will aid the productivity of your body's functions
for optimal healing and health.

SERPENTINE

for Regenerating the Body

Serpentine is an exceptional tool for awakening vital energy in your body and connecting you to nature on a profound level.

DESCRIPTION   Can range in color from yellow-green to dark green, sometimes containing black- and green-hued splotches.

WHERE TO USE IT   Bury serpentine in your outdoor spaces, either in the garden or inside of potted plants, to stimulate their growth.

WHERE IT'S FOUND   Serpentine is commonly found in the United Kingdom, China, South Africa, and the United States.

SPIRITUAL GROWTH POWERS   Kundalini awakening, creativity, one with nature. Working with serpentine can help you create deep bonds with nature, animals, and insects. Meditating with this crystal can lead you to understanding your place within the greater scope of the world.

PHYSICAL HEALING POWERS   Serpentine is a tool for replenishing energy and has been known to help people suffering from diabetes and parasites.

CHAKRA   All. Serpentine stimulates your kundalini energy (a form of primal, sacred energy that resides within you) and can be used to clear out blockages and activate all chakras. While laying down, place a piece of serpentine on your crown and root chakra points to experience a surge in vital energy.

PURPOSE AND FUNCTION

Serpentine is extremely powerful for activating kundalini energy in your body. Named for its serpentlike color, this smooth green crystal can help clear up blockages in the body that lead to poor health and disease. Also prized for the way it encourages cell regeneration, serpentine is reported to be tremendously helpful for those experiencing the effects of diabetes, calcium and magnesium deficiency, as well as parasites in the body. When utilizing this stone for its kundalini activation ability, be prepared for an almost flamelike heat to roll through your body. This is a potent crystal for sexual stimulation and energy, made even more powerful when paired with tektite, tiger's eye, or red jasper.

Serpentine is also notorious for its abilities to help you communicate with nature and animals and embrace a feeling of oneness with the outdoors. If you live in an urban, concrete-jungle type environment, invest in a few of these for your workspace and get a charge of natural wonder.

MANTRA

I utilize the energy and beauty of nature
to recharge my mind and body.

Repeating this with your serpentine crystal in hand
will connect you with the natural world around you
and provide you with cellular healing.

MOONSTONE

for Goddess Energy

Moonstone is also known as a stone of feminine mystery and is powerfully tied to fertility and hormonal balance in women.

DESCRIPTION   Its color ranges through shades of white, blue, peach, and gray, containing a moonlike sheen with flashes of color throughout.

WHERE TO USE IT   Place this crystal wherever you desire more relaxation. Gently roll it over your stomach during menstrual periods. Keep a small tumbled piece in your pocket to keep your chakras balanced.

WHERE IT'S FOUND   A mainstay for rituals since ancient Rome and a popular gem for jewelry during the early 1900s, this dreamy and smooth stone is **primarily** sourced in India, Sri Lanka, Australia, and the United States.

SPIRITUAL GROWTH POWERS   Goddess energy, intuition, control, protection. Moonstone is helpful for instilling a sense of peace and patience while you go through the ebbs and flows of your life. Helping project hidden truths and divine power, this crystal passes on sacred and mysterious feminine energy to unlock your inner goddess. It's also reported to be a powerful ally if you are doing past-life regression work.

PHYSICAL HEALING POWERS   Moonstone can help the growth of children and teens as well as slow the aging process of the elderly. Historically, this crystal has primarily been used as a conduit of feminine-goddess energy for fertility and during childbirth and menstruation. Moonstone is also a wonderful aid for balancing hormones in the body.

CHAKRA   Crown. Rest the stone in your lap or hold it in your hand to activate this chakra.

PURPOSE AND FUNCTION

Moonstone is considered to hold the power of mystery within it. This stone can grow intuition, instill patience, and amplify feelings of peace. Often used for journeys that take you inward, this crystal has a strong tie to the moon and to the rhythms of earth's natural energies. Harnessing sacred feminine/goddess energy, this crystal is considered the ultimate tool for fertility and awakening sexual desire. It's also a very useful tool for balancing hormones, menstrual pain relief, and water retention.

Though widely used for female issues, moonstone can be a beautiful tool for men, too, as it helps them become more in tune with their own divine feminine energy and encourages emotional balance.

MANTRA

I open myself to the power of the sacred goddess energy that resides within me.

Repeating this with your moonstone crystal in hand
will help you embrace and utilize the stabilizing
feminine energy inside of you for balance and intuition.

CARNELIAN

for Supreme Vitality

Carnelian is a stone of action and vibrant passion, most often used for accelerated healing and increased vitality.

DESCRIPTION   Fiery orange-red with a vibrant inner glow.

WHERE TO USE IT   Carnelian uses its fire energy to bring passion to the spaces it is in. Place it near the front door for protection and a welcoming of abundance. Keep a small piece with you when feeling ill for accelerated healing. If you're looking to add passion in the bedroom, keep it near the bed during intimacy—though be careful to remove it from the area before falling asleep because carnelian's powerful energy can interrupt your sleep.

WHERE IT'S FOUND   Natural carnelian has become more of a rarity on the commercial market. Much of what is sold is actually dyed/heat-treated agate (stripes are a giveaway it is not natural). The largest amounts of carnelian are found in India. It is often also sourced from Peru, Brazil, and the United States.

SPIRITUAL GROWTH POWERS   Revitalizing, sexual energy, pleasure, courage. Carnelian is a crystal that helps you manifest your destiny with bold, motivated action. Meditation with this stone will help you break through limiting thoughts and find the path to bring your ideas to fruition. It can also be used for protection against envy, jealousy, and negative emotions.

PHYSICAL HEALING POWERS   Carnelian helps fight fatigue and laziness, lending its abilities to a feeling of intense energy and vitality. Its vibration makes it a great help when you experience feelings of apathy or depression. Ancient Greeks and Romans often wore this stone as protection against sin, though in modern times we think of it as encouraging willpower and detoxing the body of alcohol and drugs.

CHAKRA   Root, sacral, solar plexus. Activate these areas by rubbing a polished piece of carnelian that has been lightly heated with warm water in a circular motion on your chakra points.

PURPOSE AND FUNCTION

Carnelian brings with it a powerful vibration of vitality, sexual energy, and bold action. This is considered to be a great stone for accelerated healing and general good health, in addition to a powerful ally for balancing your body's energy. This crystal is all about action; getting your body and mind moving with a surge of vital energy so that you can heal yourself on a physical level and accomplish your goals on a mental one. Carnelian is great for metabolism, vitamin absorption, balancing the genitals, regeneration of tissues, issues of the thyroid, and cleansing the blood. It can also be extremely helpful in detoxing from alcohol and drug use.

Because of its strong ability to bring the energy of acceleration into your life, carnelian has been known to help in areas of love as well and can be used as a tool for reigniting passion and romance. I like to call carnelian my "Monday stone," as I often carry it for a burst of energy and confidence as I start each week.

———◆———

MANTRA

I am filled with vital energy and begin each day feeling fully rested and restored.

Repeating this with your carnelian crystal in hand will energize your body and mind while filling you with confidence and bold action.

HEMATITE
for Building Strength

Hematite is a powerful tool for strengthening the body and protecting your spiritual life, often used as a conduit for manifesting your desires.

DESCRIPTION   Shiny steel gray to metallic black in color. Can also be magnetic.

WHERE TO USE IT   When placed in the corners of a room, hematite can create a protective spiritual grid. This is a great stone to keep with you regularly for its grounding energy. For feng shui practices, look for hematite that is carved into the shapes of animals. This stone is quite popular as jewelry, specifically in the form of a ring.

WHERE IT'S FOUND   Though hematite can also be found in colors like rusty red and brown, for commercial use, it is primarily steel gray or metallic black. This stone is commonly sourced in Canada, Brazil, the United Kingdom, Italy, and Switzerland.

SPIRITUAL GROWTH POWERS   Grounding, manifestation, healing. This stone is strongly linked to blending your physical life with your spiritual life. It is able to dissolve negativity and help you find the lessons you are meant to learn. Hematite helps boost self-esteem and enhances both willpower and survivability. Meditate with this stone to bring concentration and calming energy to your mind.

PHYSICAL HEALING POWERS   Hematite is best used to help strengthen the blood supply, support blood production, and encourage the formation of red blood cells because of its high iron content. It can also aid with detoxification and perform as a cleanser for the liver and kidneys. This stone can ease the pain from back issues (vertebrae, spleen, aches), as well as fractures or broken bones. Place a piece of polished hematite at the top and base of the spine while laying down for healing in that area.

CHAKRA   Root. Because hematite is strongly connected to the healing and strengthening of the back and spine, placing a stone on your root chakra will activate this area for balancing and healing.

PURPOSE AND FUNCTION

Named from the Greek word *haima*, which translates to "blood," hematite is a stone with a high iron content and a deeply rooted history of strength. According to legend, Native Americans used powdered hematite as war paint and deposits of this shiny mineral have been formed in places where battles were fought due to bloodshed seeping into the earth. This crystal has long been used for its spiritual healing properties of manifestation and grounding. Known to help lead you toward more self-confidence, emotional strength, and courage, working with this stone can bring protection to your home and your spiritual journey. Its reputation for "keeping you grounded" comes from its energetic ability to strengthen your connection to the earth. Using hematite has also been recorded as a tremendous help to the kidneys and the liver by promoting detoxification in those organs.

A fortifier of blood, using hematite is very beneficial when experiencing issues like anemia, blood clots, and period cramping. Working with this crystal is very beneficial for both men and women. While a girlfriend of mine swears by wearing a hematite ring during her cycle every month to ward off painful cramps, I find myself rolling my egg-sized tumbled version over my lower back after workouts to calm the muscles and keep an old injury from flaring up.

MANTRA

In all moments, my body and spirit are grounded and radiate strength.

Repeating this with your hematite stone in hand brings you grounding energy and combines your physical and spiritual lives.

10.

Crystals for Mental Health

Mental health affects how you think, how you feel, and how you act. In every stage of your life, from childhood to elderhood, your mental health is intrinsically linked with the quality of life you live. When your mental health is balanced, it allows you to be productive, create impact, build meaningful relationships, cope with the stress of daily life, and fully walk inside of your purpose. Recent studies have found that living more mindfully can have a dramatically positive effect on your mental health.

How do you know if your mental health could use a little help? Just pay attention to the signs. Depression, anxiety, mood swings, low energy, emotional numbness, self-isolation, destructive behavior, and harmful thoughts are just a few of the signs that appear when it's time to devote more energy to yourself. For me, feelings of restlessness and depression are what initially led me to the world of crystal healing. I needed a boost of energy and some subtle direction. Through crystal work, self-care, and meditation, I forever changed the quality of my life for the better. Using stones like lepidolite to get rid of anxiety or fluorite for enhancing your ability to make great decisions, the vibrations of healing crystal energy can be just what you need to invigorate your mind and bring peace to your thoughts. In Chapter 10, I will introduce you to five beautiful stones to add to your collection for enhanced mental health. Time to unwind!

FLUORITE
for a Focused Mind

Fluorite is a powerful stone for activating the mind and enhancing focus, as well as good decision-making, by clearing you of confusion and cleansing your chakras.

DESCRIPTION Fluorite comes in a wide variety of colors, like purple, green, yellow, blue, pink, and red. Often naturally found in the shapes of a cube or octahedron, this crystal has the ability to glow brightly under UV light.

WHERE TO USE IT Keep fluorite close by when working on your computer for enhanced concentration, as well as to clear electromagnetic stress. Place it around framed family photos to help mend poor relationships. Keep a piece of raw fluorite in the heart of your home to promote understanding.

WHERE IT'S FOUND Alternately referred to as "fluor spar," fluorite is commonly found in China, South Africa, Mexico, the United States, and the United Kingdom.

SPIRITUAL GROWTH POWERS Focus. Decision making. Meditation. Concentration. Fluorite helps heighten/grow your intuition and provide powerful psychic protection. Meditate with fluorite when needing to focus the mind, tap into your subconscious, and/or distinguish your true feelings on something free from outside chatter or manipulations.

PHYSICAL HEALING POWERS   Though prized for its ability to help brain activity and memory, fluorite is also very beneficial as a strengthener of bones and teeth and as a pain reliever for those suffering from arthritis. It can also be helpful when battling colds, the flu, infections, or viruses, as well as when trying to maintain your weight or as protection against eating disorders.

CHAKRA   All. Though fluorite is connected to all chakras, keeping this stone in hand helps to specifically activate your throat and crown chakras, as well as cleanse and balance your aura.

PURPOSE AND FUNCTION

Fluorite is a powerful tool to help clear your life of negativity and confusion. Known for its ability to organize and align chaotic energy, working with this crystal can lead to better decision-making, as well as enhanced focus. Concentration is the name of the game for this stone. Of course, this lends itself to expanded opportunity in your work life but an even bigger perk of utilizing fluorite is its ability to calm your mind and remove stressful thoughts so that you can make the choices that serve your highest good on a spiritual level.

"What do I really want?" That's a question we often repeat to ourselves as we journey through this world. When you work with and meditate with fluorite, that question effortlessly begins to answer itself and manifest in your daily life. It's also a wonderful tool for protection against psychic attack, as well as a cleansing agent for your aura and chakras. When you regularly surround yourself with this uniquely shaped crystal, you will experience mental freedom and enhanced strategic thinking. Carry it often!

MANTRA

My mind is clear and I am able to make choices
that serve my highest good with ease.

Repeating this with your fluorite crystal in hand will
cleanse your chakras and sharpen your mind.

TREE AGATE

for a Positive Outlook

Tree agate, sometimes known as "dendritic agate," is a powerful tool used for easing mental stress and creating shifts in perspective and ego.

DESCRIPTION White with green tree branch-like patterns.

WHERE TO USE IT Because of its mild vibration, place this crystal in any part of your home that could benefit from a calming and gentle energy.

WHERE IT'S FOUND First found on the Italian island of Sicily, tree agate is now commonly sourced in India.

SPIRITUAL GROWTH POWERS Growth, stability, wisdom, grounding. Tree agate is helpful for breaking patterns and lovingly changing the perception you have of yourself. Meditate with this stone to release ego-driven, comparative behaviors, which can be the root cause for feelings of mental anguish.

PHYSICAL HEALING POWERS Tree agate is helpful for healing the body in areas that resemble branches like the skeletal system, nerves, and blood vessels. Very calming and soothing to the mind, this crystal helps clear tension, stagnant energy, and stress.

CHAKRA Heart. Hold this crystal against your heart and breathe deeply with your eyes closed, visualizing white light being exchanged between it and you to activate this chakra.

PURPOSE AND FUNCTION

In general, agates have been thought to operate at a slower vibrational frequency than other healing crystals. It's important to know that in this case, slower does not mean less powerful. Agate energy is extremely strengthening, and when you work with it, it can provide a lasting and firm vibration. Very different in appearance from others in this crystal family, tree agate is named for its tree branch–like inclusions and imprints. This crystal is a powerful tool for breaking familiar patterns that seem to be repeating in your life. Over time, working with this stone will extinguish the self-destructive behavior that you engage in, freeing you of toxic and unfounded feelings of shame, guilt, and jealousy.

Tree agate also helps you find the gift in the obstacles you face, allowing you to walk away from experiences with a positive view on even the most difficult life lessons. This crystal can be especially helpful for those who have experienced mental- and ego-based traumas. When using this stone, be prepared to do some spiritual heavy lifting in your life. The self-work has to be there in order for this crystal to work at its best.

MANTRA

I view myself through the eyes of the divine
and not through the eyes of my ego.

Repeating this with your tree agate crystal in hand will help you break away from self-destructive thoughts and behaviors.

BLOODSTONE

for Peace During Adversity

Also referred to as "heliotrope" or "Christ stone," bloodstone is a useful ally during times of change and is a powerful tool for calming aggression.

DESCRIPTION   Deep forest green with splatters and swirls of burgundy red.

WHERE TO USE IT   Keep bloodstone near you as a companion when experiencing times of change and mental stress. Display in the work or study area of your home. It's also a helpful addition to your first aid kit.

WHERE IT'S FOUND   A member of the jasper family, bloodstone is typically found in India, China, and Australia.

SPIRITUAL GROWTH POWERS   Emotional balance, courage, endurance, altruism. Meditate with it to bring calm when adjusting to large-scale change.

PHYSICAL HEALING POWERS   Many thousands of years ago, this crystal was powdered and mixed with honey as a cure against snake venom and even tumors. Today, as its name would suggest, bloodstone is considered to be a great healer for blood-related ailments like hemorrhages, anemia, nosebleeds, menstrual bleeding, and issues of blood clotting. This stone is also useful for removing toxins and addressing hormone imbalances.

CHAKRA   Root and heart. Activate these chakras by placing your bloodstone crystal on the base of your spine while laying face down, or place it on top of your heart space while laying down face up. This will help clear blockages and increase stamina.

PURPOSE AND FUNCTION

A member of the jasper family, bloodstone has a deep connection to the Christian religion. In the Middle Ages, this crystal was referred to as "Christ stone" and was said to have been formed during the crucifixion of Jesus, when his blood fell from the cross and seeped into the green earth. This stone brings with it an energy of endurance and courage and is very useful when used during difficult times of mental distress and emotional imbalance. Bloodstone is a great tool for clearing chakra blockages that can stagnate your energy flow and bring down your emotional, mental, and physical energies. Use this crystal for added courage in the face of obstacles and a mental boost of confidence.

It can also be extremely helpful for those who are easily triggered and prone to aggression, because working with bloodstone provides emotional balance, self-control, and calming energy.

MANTRA

I exude an energy of strength and calm while experiencing moments of change.

Repeating this with your bloodstone crystal in hand will provide nurturing confidence and a peaceful outlook as you experience shifts in your life.

BLUE LACE AGATE

for Attunement

Blue lace agate is a great tool for communicating spiritual ideas and calming those who are mentally overstimulated.

DESCRIPTION   A mix of pale sky-blue and white with a banded (layered) appearance.

WHERE TO USE IT   Because of its mild vibration, place this crystal in any part of your home that could benefit from a calming and gentle energy. It's useful as a calming agent for an overstimulated mind when placed under your pillow at night.

WHERE IT'S FOUND   This member of the banded agate family is almost exclusively sourced from South Africa.

SPIRITUAL GROWTH POWERS   Attunement, balance, clarity, communication. This is a great stone to work with for communicating spiritual ideas and discerning the truth in matters where the lines between reality and imagination may be skewed. It can also help bring you spiritual attunement. Meditate with this stone to help manifest new methods of growth and expression.

PHYSICAL HEALING POWERS   Blue lace agate is a great stone for calming anxiety and soothing a tired mind. Its connection to the throat chakra makes its physical healing properties especially beneficial to healing laryngitis, sore throat, and speech issues. (Wear it around the neck, choker style, to accelerate healing for these ailments.) This crystal can also alleviate skin issues like eczema because of its overall soothing energy.

CHAKRA   Throat. Wear high up around the neck or sip in water elixir form to activate this chakra.

PURPOSE AND FUNCTION

Blue lace agate, with its beautiful banded patterns of blue, white, and sometimes lavender, has been popular in décor and jewelry for centuries. This crystal helps enhance mental function and encourages deep spiritual understanding and growth. The calming and balancing energy that this crystal brings helps soothe overactive minds and imaginations. It is often recommended for children who have problems falling asleep and telling lies.

In general, agates have been thought to operate at a slower vibrational frequency than other crystals. In this case, slower does not mean less powerful. Agate energy is extremely strengthening and it can provide a lasting and firm vibration. Its flow of even energy can help bring harmony to the minds of busy parents and households. It's a great gift for new moms and dads!

MANTRA
I stand in my truth and communicate
my beliefs effortlessly.

Repeating this with your blue lace agate crystal in hand will bring you spiritual attunement and ease of communication.

LEPIDOLITE

for Overcoming Anxiety

This purple powerhouse can help you push through paralyzing anxiety and bring you enhanced mental abilities.

DESCRIPTION   Lavender with patches of pink, purple, gray, and yellow. Often scaly in texture.

WHERE TO USE IT   Keep lepidolite under your pillow for peaceful sleep and positive dreaming. Place a piece of this crystal on the counter in your bathroom for help with your digestion and when experiencing constipation.

WHERE IT'S FOUND   One of the softest and most delicate crystals used commercially, lepidolite can be found in the United States, Africa, and Brazil.

SPIRITUAL GROWTH POWERS   Knowledge, relaxation, transition. Lepidolite is a stone that can greatly help you live a life of enhanced joy, peace, and love. Meditation with this stone will help you subconsciously work through feelings of depression, stress, and emotional transition.

PHYSICAL HEALING POWERS   Lepidolite is extremely helpful for those suffering from mental and emotional imbalances. Providing a stabilizing energy against anxiety and depression, this crystal can also help enhance mental understanding and memory functions. Lepidolite has also been reported as a great help for digestion and constipation. When used as part of your beauty regimen, it can also help delay wrinkles from forming.

Massage your face with a tumbled lepidolite crystal or place two small pieces over your eyelids for a few moments before bed to enjoy its beauty benefits.

CHAKRA   Heart and third eye. Place this stone on your forehead while resting to activate these chakras and create a flow of good energy.

PURPOSE AND FUNCTION

Lepidolite is a potent tool for removing stress, calming nerves, and easing anxiety. Helping you ease symptoms of depression by encouraging momentary surrender to the sadness, it can also help you shift your perspective by showing you the beauty in experiencing difficulty. Feelings of anxiety and depression are almost exclusively fear-based. By working with lepidolite, you are covered with vibrations of grace and surrender, which will help you learn how to free yourself of the limiting thoughts and behaviors that lead to mental and emotional suffering. This has long been one of my favorite stones to place in the Karma Bliss bags because its energy lends itself to mental and emotional freedom—which is extremely beneficial no matter what your journey.

MANTRA

I experience life's ups and downs with an even flow of energy and a peaceful outlook.

Repeating this with your lepidolite can remove anxiety, fear, and stress from your mind and encourage your surrender to the moment.

11.

Crystals for Spiritual Growth and Healing

You know what can give you an all-around accelerated pathway to living a better life? Spiritual growth. Though it requires a lifelong commitment and lots of hard work, choosing to grow spiritually and heal from your past is almost like a cheat code to reaching your dreams and experiencing success.

Often, I find myself acting as an unofficial therapist for my friends. One day, while talking to a kindred spirit who had been extremely depressed and self-sabotaging over experiences from his childhood, it hit me like a ton of bricks how feeling good can actually be a choice. As we talked about what he was dealing with, he kept saying the same thing over and over—dealing with those feelings was "too hard." It occurred to me as he said that, that either path we choose (dealing or denial and repeating a cycle) is difficult, but at least the growing pains from healing have a payoff, while the other path keeps you locked into the same feeling, forever. Eventually, through much soul searching and a few crystal gifts from me, my friend thankfully found his way back to himself.

When we choose to embark on the path of the seeker, utilizing the healing properties of crystals can guide us in a much gentler and productive direction. Working with crystals like amethyst or black obsidian can be indescribably valuable in protecting you and helping you uncover deeper meanings as you heal and grow spiritually. Chapter 11 will provide you with five stones that can take you to the next level spiritually. Let's get growing!

AMETHYST

for Connecting with the Divine

Amethyst is a powerful tool for facilitating spiritual awareness and protection during spiritual exploration.

DESCRIPTION Light violet to deep mauve and can be found in various forms like banded masses, geodes, and gem-quality crystal clusters.

WHERE TO USE IT Wear amethyst jewelry as protection against addictive behavior and use in all areas of your home for a feeling of stability and support.

WHERE IT'S FOUND One of the most popular gems in the world, amethyst is commonly found in Mexico, Africa, Canada, Russia, and Brazil.

SPIRITUAL GROWTH POWERS Releasing addictions, overcoming fears, divine communication, wisdom. Meditate with amethyst to unveil the unseen motives and reasons behind your behavior. This beautiful crystal provides a calming effect that helps to defend against stress and negative energy and encourages you to take action toward finding supportive and stable environments in which to grow.

PHYSICAL HEALING POWERS Often incorporated in treatments for alcohol and drug addictions, working with amethyst can also help with addictions to food and gambling. This is also a great crystal for strengthening the immune system and bringing balance to the brain and nervous system.

Place a piece of amethyst under your pillow to help with insomnia and rub a tumbled or polished piece on your forehead to dissipate headaches.

CHAKRA Third eye and crown. Hold amethyst in your hand and gaze into it, imagining white light radiating from it to activate your chakras.

PURPOSE AND FUNCTION

Amethyst has the ability to surround you with a light of protection as it encourages spiritual exploration and self-discovery. Working with this stone helps foster and grow your intuition and your psychic abilities. Working with this stone can be extremely powerful as it helps you learn how to surrender to your higher power and connect with sacred and divine energy. When using this stone, expect to have many "aha" moments, as it creates a free-flowing pathway between you and the divine energy of the universe so that you may uncover the deepest parts of who you are.

MANTRA

I surrender myself to the divine will of the universe.

Repeating this with your amethyst crystal in hand will help you discover a deeper spiritual path and surrender to the unknown.

SPIRIT QUARTZ
for Spiritual Evolution

Spirit quartz is a powerful tool for facilitating your spiritual evolution so you may live as your highest self.

DESCRIPTION Hues range from colorless to violet and rusty yellow-brown. Has a cactus-like appearance, with a single crystal point that is covered in clusters of small points.

WHERE TO USE IT Because of its beauty and unique shape, this is a wonderful stone to use as a display piece in your home. Place in your meditation or relaxation area to access your subconscious energies.

WHERE IT'S FOUND Also referred to by some retailers as "cactus quartz," due to its appearance, this unique and beautiful crystal is exclusively found in South Africa.

SPIRITUAL GROWTH POWERS Fearlessness, becoming highest self, rebirth. This stone is amazing for release of stagnant and painful emotions that have haunted you in this life and any past lives. Meditate with this stone to gain access to and release subconscious thoughts and feelings that may be hindering your spiritual growth.

PHYSICAL HEALING POWERS A great stone for general healing and balancing energy, spirit quartz has also been thought to be of assistance to those with fertility issues.

CHAKRA   Crown. Meditating with and holding spirit quartz will activate your crown chakra and balance your aura.

PURPOSE AND FUNCTION

Spirit quartz, one of the most unique-looking stones in the crystal world, is also one of the most powerful. Though its name stems from a coincidence (its color represents a cleaning solution used in South Africa called "spirit"), it fits its healing properties perfectly. Working with this stone gives you a sense of belonging; a desire to grow yourself emotionally and spiritually for your own good and for the role you play in the lives of others. You will notice a greater understanding of how your life fits in relation to other people's lives. Spirit quartz represents spiritual ascension. It consolidates the version of who you are now and your highest self as it encourages you to release past pain.

This crystal is also extremely helpful as a supportive tool during times of grief and fear. Working with this stone gives you access to the entirety of who you are; the trinity of past, present, and future, as well as the contrasting sides of light and dark. I love to gift it to friends—especially those who have recently started meditating. It makes for a great necklace if you tie a suede cord or braided linen around it!

MANTRA

*I embrace the entirety of who I am so that
I may evolve into my highest self.*

Repeating this with your spirit quartz will lead you toward spiritual evolution and help you release painful past experiences.

ANGELITE

for Aligning with Your Angels

Angelite is a high-vibration stone that can increase your ability to communicate with the angel realm and receive guidance from your spiritual guardians.

DESCRIPTION   A calming soft blue that is often seen with cloudy white swirls and inclusions. This crystal often forms in the shape of nuggets and large masses.

WHERE TO USE IT   Sleep with this stone under your pillow for dream recall and communication with your angels while sleeping. Hold it in your palm during meditation to gently harness its healing properties.

WHERE IT'S FOUND   Also known as "blue anhydrite," angelite is exclusively found in Peru.

SPIRITUAL GROWTH POWERS   Security, healing, serenity, angels. This highly protective stone supports communication with the spirit realm and is especially helpful for leading you to your guardians, angels, and spirit animals. Meditate with this crystal to gain clear directions you should take and insight into who/what is guiding you.

PHYSICAL HEALING POWERS   Angelite is great for your skeletal structure and helps heal broken bones and fractures. The energy of this crystal can also be used as an appetite suppressant and aid in digestion. Use as a skin essence to repel insects.

CHAKRA Throat. Use topically as an essence (rubbed over the throat)/ ingest as a drink or hold in hand to activate this chakra and enhance communication on all levels.

PURPOSE AND FUNCTION

Angelite's name is a clear giveaway of its beautiful and supportive healing properties. Angel communication, guardian communication, and identification of your spirit animals are experiences that are possible when working with this crystal. The energy of this crystal extends itself to enhancing your compassion and ability to peacefully navigate conflict. Its soothing energy can be specifically wonderful for those suffering from grief or prone to anger and emotional outbursts.

One of my girlfriends found this stone to be incredibly supportive as she delved deeper into her religious practice and wore an index finger ring made of this beautiful stone. I myself have carried it on me when dieting and often noticed a feeling of fullness in my body during the day. As you can tell, this little rock is useful for many things!

MANTRA

I allow myself to be led by the loving and compassionate wisdom of my angels.

Repeating this with your angelite crystal in hand will connect you with the guides and angels that stay near you.

KYANITE

for Deep Emotional Healing

Kyanite offers powerful emotional healing through self-examination and intuitive guidance.

DESCRIPTION   Sky blue with a translucent pearly sheen. It's often shaped like long, flat blades, and can be flaky to the touch.

WHERE TO USE IT   Keep kyanite with you as jewelry or a touchstone when speaking publicly or leading group activities. For lucid dreaming, sleep with kyanite under your pillow.

WHERE IT'S FOUND   Found in blue, black, pink, white, and green, kyanite is commonly sourced in Brazil, Mexico, and Switzerland.

SPIRITUAL GROWTH POWERS   Perseverance, fairness, emotional healing. Kyanite is a wonderful tool for discernment and clearing energy blockages from emotional pain. If it was possible to taste its energy, it would taste like freedom. Meditate with this crystal to experience yin-yang balance.

PHYSICAL HEALING POWERS   Kyanite is a great stone for the brain and the throat. For this reason, it is especially good for singers and those in leadership positions. Use this crystal for healing of brain/head trauma.

CHAKRA   All. Simply place on any of your seven chakra points to feel those areas being cleared.

PURPOSE AND FUNCTION

Kyanite is an incredible crystal for emotional healing and experiencing feelings of wholeness. It helps create energy bridges that allow you to cross over painful emotions that have kept you stagnant and stuck. Kyanite cannot contain or accumulate negative energy, so this is one of the few stones that never needs cleansing (which is great news since this crystal should not be soaked in water, due to its delicate makeup. If it gets dirty, you can dampen a cloth with water and gently wipe it down.) and can be used to charge other crystals in your collection simply by placing them next to this stone.

On a subtle level, working with this stone helps free energy blockages and cut through patterns of self-destruction, negative self-talk, and emotional masochism. This stone provides the same type of relief that you'd feel if the chains that were binding you were broken and you could live freely once more. When I am able to find small-sized pieces of this blade-like crystal, I love to include them as free gifts in the orders I receive on KarmaBliss.com because I feel that this is a stone that absolutely everyone can benefit from.

MANTRA

I walk through the fire of my pain to experience freedom thanks to healing.

Repeating this with your kyanite crystal in hand will support you as you visit and release the emotional pain you are carrying to become whole.

BLACK OBSIDIAN

for Facing Your Inner Darkness

Also known as "Apache tear," black obsidian is a volcanic glass that helps you face unpleasant truths so you can work through and release them.

DESCRIPTION Glossy black and glasslike in appearance and texture with sharp edges.

WHERE TO USE IT Use when experiencing emotional hardship by holding it or placing it under your pillow while you sleep. Place a larger piece near the front and bedroom doors of your home to stop negativity before it enters these spaces. Because it draws negative energy in, cleanse regularly.

WHERE IT'S FOUND A member of the vast volcanic rock obsidian family, black obsidian is primarily found in Mexico and the United States.

SPIRITUAL GROWTH POWERS Grounding, protection, release of past. Black obsidian can give you the strength to stand on your own and release limiting thoughts that have kept you viewing life from a place of lack. By bringing negative feelings and unpleasant truths to the forefront, this crystal helps you work through and release them. Meditation with this crystal reveals opportunities to confront past experiences and slay your dragons.

PHYSICAL HEALING POWERS Black obsidian strengthens the body's organs and helps the detoxification process, aiding in digestion, and the dissolving of blockages. It can help clear blockages in the reproductive system as well. When placed under your bed or pillow, this stone can help draw out stress and tension.

CHAKRA   Root. Though connected to the root chakra, obsidian is wonderful for clearing blockages to the third eye and solar plexus chakras. Place black obsidian on the navel or forehead to activate these chakras.

PURPOSE AND FUNCTION

Also referred to as "Apache tear," this glasslike volcanic rock got that name from an 1800s legend. It has been said that after many brave Apache leapt to their deaths after being outnumbered by the US Cavalry, the tears of their loved ones turned to black stone as they fell. Working with this stone helps you face your inner demons (or darkness) and accept those facets of self in order to release them and remove the shame of having had them. It helps your perspective shift from a place of hiding unpleasant aspects of who you are or pain from previous experiences to a place of acceptance and gratitude. Using this stone for emotional healing can be extremely powerful, so be gentle with yourself as you work with this rock.

MANTRA

I bravely face the entirety of who I am with honesty, integrity, and self-acceptance.

Repeating this with your black obsidian rock in hand will help you face your inner darkness and integrate it into your life.

Part Three

FURTHERING YOUR CRYSTAL JOURNEY

Now that you are fully entrenched in the beautiful world of crystal healing, it's time to take you to the next level! There are many stones and tools in the metaphysical world that can enhance the crystal work and spiritual journeying you are already doing. Rituals that have been used for thousands of years, like smudging or playing a singing bowl, can keep your energy balanced and protected. Likewise, understanding your chakras can aid in keeping you in alignment, making crystal essence elixirs will intensify your energy, and adding meteorites and shamanic stones to your crystal collection can enhance the power of your crystal healing work. Over the next few chapters we will delve into the next steps you can take to further your journey in the world of crystals!

12.

Enhancement Crystals and Other Tools

All of the stones we have gone over so far in this book offer incredible healing properties and can bring you beautiful energy to manifest all of your heart's desires. And while their vibrations are whole all by themselves, adding a few companion crystals into the equation can really amplify your experiences as you work with crystal healing. Some crystals operate at such a high frequency that when paired with another stone, they exhibit remarkable transformational power.

My first experience with moldavite, a piece of meteor (or "space crystal" as it's sometimes called), gave me a glimpse into the true power of amplifier stones. As I put it in my hand along with an amethyst crystal and sliver of stibnite, I felt my heart rate speed up, and I started to sweat. I kept that combination with me for a few hours every day, and I noticed a shift happening in the way I was experiencing my meditation, as well as in my interactions with others. Amethyst's ability to uncover root issues behind behavior patterns and connect me to the universe's divine energy was more clear than ever when paired with another enhancement crystal.

In this chapter are five of my favorite enhancement stones. You will also learn some of the most enthralling scents and sounds you can use to clear out negativity!

MOLDAVITE
for Rapid Transformation

Moldavite is a tremendous tool for spiritual activation and transformation.

DESCRIPTION   Ranging in hue from pale green to deep emerald green and usually only available in small shards and pieces, moldavite has a feathered and branch-like glass appearance and feel.

USE WITH   All crystals. It's especially powerful when paired with amethyst, citrine, spirit quartz, and nuumite.

WHERE IT'S FOUND   Close to 15 million years ago, a meteor hit earth with a tremendous impact, creating a melted material that is today known as moldavite. The Czech Republic is the sole place this space gem exists.

CHAKRA   All. The energetic vibrations of moldavite can activate and clear blockages for all chakras. Hold it in your hand or touch it to different chakra areas to achieve this.

PURPOSE AND FUNCTION

Moldavite has been used as jewelry and for its energetic properties for thousands of years. This green powerhouse, also known as green tektite, is part earth and part space, making it a useful tool for accelerated spiritual growth and higher consciousness. The reaction each person has to this stone is different. Moldavite carries an intense vibration and makes many people feel dizzy and hot when touching it for the first time. It is highly recommended to ease into working with this stone and to wear it sparingly so that you can gradually adapt to its energy. As I have shared earlier in this chapter, my first experience holding moldavite left me with flushed cheeks and cold sweats.

One of the first crystals I began working with, I credit moldavite with helping me have a greater understanding of myself and creating synchronistic (a concept of meaningful coincidences) experiences in my life that led me to opportunities for emotional and spiritual growth. This crystal is an extremely powerful tool for transformation and spiritual evolution and can help you open your mind and heart to the unlimited possibilities of the universe.

MANTRA

I am open to receiving all that is necessary for my spiritual evolution.

Repeating this with your moldavite stone in hand will lead you toward self-evolution and boost your confidence during transition.

NUUMITE

for Finding Your Personal Magic

Also known as "the sorcerer's stone," nuumite is a crystal for enhancing your personal magic and manifesting synchronicities.

DESCRIPTION   Black with gold and rainbow sparks of iridescent color.

USE WITH   Moldavite, amethyst, and amazonite. Can lead to accelerated wisdom and personal freedom when paired with lapis lazuli or rhodonite.

WHERE IT'S FOUND   This rare crystal is primarily found in Greenland and is roughly 3 billion years old.

CHAKRA   Root. Hold the stone in your hand while meditating to activate this chakra.

PURPOSE AND FUNCTION

Working with nuumite helps connect you to your inner power and manifest synchronistic opportunities for abundance in your life. This crystal provides a consistent energy of courage and self-compassion to help you boldly and optimistically do the self-work necessary to become whole and open. Nuumite is a wonderful tool for personal journeying and has the ability to bring you the power necessary to master yourself as well as an abundant flow of synchronistic opportunities. Using this beautiful stone will help you walk into the fullness of who you are meant to be and stand in your truth. Meditate with nuumite for access to parts of yourself that may have previously been lost. Wear it as jewelry to attract abundance, kindness, and adventurous experiences.

MANTRA

I am made whole by fearlessly exploring my own thoughts and feelings.

Repeating this with your nuumite crystal in hand brings you the perspective shifts and experiences necessary to enhance your personal power.

SELENITE

for Cleansing Energy

Selenite is a powerfully cleansing stone that helps clear blockages and purify energy.

DESCRIPTION   Clear or white. Can be flaky or splinter-like when touched. Often found in a rectangular, bladed, or flat shape.

USE WITH   All. This crystal is helpful for enhancing the vibrations of each stone in your crystal collection. It can also be used to cleanse other stones.

WHERE IT'S FOUND   This crystalized form of gypsum is commonly found in Mexico, Canada, and Morocco.

CHAKRA   Third eye and crown. Use this crystal like a wand to touch to different areas on your body while in a relaxed state with eyes closed to activate these chakras.

PURPOSE AND FUNCTION

A favorite for building crystal energy grids, which is the practice of placing stones in geometric patterns to direct energy. Selenite is a high-vibrating stone that brings with it a purifying and cleansing energy. It amplifies the energy of all stones in your collection and can also be used to cleanse them. Oftentimes I will place the tumbled stones I carry with me onto a flat piece of selenite to clear them each evening.

Working with this stone will bring an added dose of harmony and balance into your life. Its ability to help unify mind, body, and soul make it a favorite of healers and energy workers. Selenite is also extremely beneficial to the physical body, especially when it comes to issues of the skin (including wrinkles), menstruation, and fertility, as well as health problems associated with free radicals.

———◆———

MANTRA

I am filled with light and cleansed of harmful, negative, and stagnant energy.

Repeating this with your selenite crystal in hand will help balance and purify any energy or vibrations it comes into contact with.

SHUNGITE

for Ancient Healing

Shungite is an antioxidant powerhouse that is said to have the ability to promote good health.

DESCRIPTION   Jet black with a coal-like appearance. Genuine shungite leaves a slight black residue on your hands when touched.

USE WITH   Shungite can be used with all crystals. It's especially powerful when paired with the other enhancement crystals mentioned in this chapter: moldavite, nuumite, selenite, and gold tektite.

WHERE IT'S FOUND   How this ancient stone found its way to earth is still unclear, but the deposits we have access to are solely found in the Karelia region of Russia.

CHAKRA   All. Use as an essence in your drinking water, meditate with it, or place it on various areas of your body to activate your chakras.

PURPOSE AND FUNCTION

Shungite is old—I'm talking at least 2 billion years old. One of the most beautiful things about working with crystals is experiencing an energy that existed long before human life, and that's why shungite is considered to be one of the most powerful high-vibration stones you can work with.

Though very old, there is still presently much being learned about this stone. Scientists are not fully aware of how it was formed and theories of its origin abound—they range from an idea that it came from space to the suggestion that it was formed in now nonexistent oceans.

My first experience with shungite was similar to that of moldavite. A sensational energy took over me. However, unlike the sweats and heat that I channeled with moldavite, shungite felt like a cool wind was radiating light and energy throughout my whole body. It was overwhelming but wonderful. Working with this crystal is specifically helpful with purification. Many people infuse their drinking water with a piece of this stone to charge and cleanse it, as well as keep a tumbled stone near their cell phones as protection against electromagnetic radiation. Shungite is the only natural source of fullerenes (a powerful antioxidant), and at this moment, scientists are studying its makeup and how to use it in different functions. Energetically, it's believed that anything that can be a hazard to human health cannot exist when shungite is present. I have made this unique crystal a huge part of my healing crystal collection, using a large slab as an altar in my meditation room.

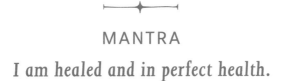

MANTRA

I am healed and in perfect health.

Repeating this with your shungite crystal in hand
can help protect and purify your body.

GOLD TEKTITE
for Manifesting Mystic Power

Gold tektite is a beautiful stone for uncovering your personal power and strengthening your will.

DESCRIPTION   Golden in color with a glassy look and feel. It's typically found as small chunks or nuggets.

USE WITH   Use with moldavite for an accelerated manifestation of your intentions. It is also advantageous to pair this with shattuckite or shiva lingam to grow your intuition and confidence. Citrine, too, pairs well for accelerating the growth of your personal power.

WHERE IT'S FOUND   Similar in makeup to moldavite, this golden, glass-like stone is exclusively found in the Sahara Desert in Egypt and Libya.

CHAKRA   All. The energetic vibrations of gold tektite can activate and clear blockages for all chakras. Hold it in your hand or touch it to different chakra areas to do this.

PURPOSE AND FUNCTION

Also known as Libyan desert glass, gold tektite is estimated to be around 26 million years old. Scientists believe it was formed from sand being exposed to thermal radiation due to a nuclear explosion (which could have been the result of a meteorite hitting earth). Its healing energies lead to a great strengthening of personal will, high levels of creativity, and manifestation of life goals. Ancient Egyptians were especially adoring of this golden power piece, often wearing it as jewelry or carving it into decorative pieces. (King Tutankhamen's tomb contained an elaborate necklace with a gold tektite carving on it.) Some even believe that the existence of this material is proof that extraterrestrials had contact with ancient Egyptians. (Watch *Ancient Aliens* for a greater understanding of this theory.) Working with gold tektite will help you become bold in your approach to life and has been known to light your creative ability on fire.

MANTRA

I boldly move through life because I understand the power I hold inside.

Repeat this with your gold tektite crystal in hand to unlock your hidden powers and help you create confidently.

SINGING BOWLS

Throughout history, singing bowls have been used all over the world as an integral part of sacred spiritual rituals, as well as for meditation, music, and personal practices. Originating in Asia, singing bowls are considered to be part of the "standing bell" family because they rest flat on the ground and emit sound when their rim is struck. They are most often used by energy workers for sound healing and sound baths. I love using singing bowls as a means to clear crystals, clear my home, and activate my chakras. The sounds emitted from running a wooden mallet over the rim of a singing bowl provides a vibrational frequency that has the power to clear negativity, balance your mind and spirit, and enhance your spiritual journey. Though singing bowls come in all shapes and sizes, many with their own harmonic frequencies, there are two particular varieties I recommend adding to your collection:

* **Tibetan Metal Singing Bowl:** This traditional piece comes with a wooden mallet and is typically made of brass (lower quality) or bell bronze (higher quality).
* **Quartz Singing Bowl:** This is more of a New Age piece and comes with a suede-wrapped mallet for striking. This beautiful and high-vibration type of singing bowl is made by heat-treating tiny quartz grains inside a special mold.

HOW TO PLAY A SINGING BOWL

Begin by lightly striking the rim of the bowl three times (think of the sound as "ding...ding...ding") and then glide the mallet along on the outer rim of the bowl. Move the mallet in a full circle around the bowl's rim at a comfortable pace; not too fast and not too slow. The sound will start faintly and then increase and grow to become more intense as you continue, coming into resonance with your own vibrations. You can play your singing bowl as often as you like. It can be a beautifully centering practice to enjoy daily if you have the time.

SMUDGING

Smudging is an ancient practice that uses the smoke of bundled herbs as an energy purifier. As we discussed in Chapter 2, smudging your crystals with a sage bundle, palo santo wood, or incense is a great way to save time as you cleanse them and clear out negativity or pre-programming.

PURCHASING SMUDGING BUNDLES

Sage smudging bundles are pretty easy to find these days at healthy retailers like Whole Foods or on Etsy. The following is more information about the most common types of smudging bundles:

* **Copal:** Made of a resin found in copal trees in Mexico, its purifying and earthy scent has been used for clearing negative energy since the ancient Mayan civilization. Copal has an extremely purifying and grounding scent and can be found in stick and rock form in many specialty shops or with a quick search on Amazon.
* **Palo Santo Wood:** Made from the wood of the palo santo trees in South America, and considered "holy wood" by healers and shamans, it provides a fresh and sweet scent when lit. Palo santo wood can be found at most New Age stores and many healthy and hipster retailers as well. I love including pieces of this fragrant wood as a thank-you gift in orders for patrons of my site KarmaBliss.com.

* **Sage:** A delicious herb used for cooking, perfumes, and candles, sage becomes a powerfully aromatic cleansing agent with a pungent warm and herbaceous scent when dried. You can even easily create your own bundles with dried green or white sage bound together with a thin piece of cotton string.

SMUDGING YOUR HOME

Smudging is also a wonderful ritual to do on yourself or in any space you inhabit, as it also has the ability to cleanse the energy and remove any negativity that you yourself may be carrying or that may inhabit the room or space you are in. The smoke acts as a purifying agent and can engulf, transform, and remove any bad energy. I like to smudge my home at least once a quarter (and after any parties, gatherings, or arguments) by lighting sage, palo santo wood, or copal incense and traveling from room to room as I use a feather to waft the smoke around the air. You can do this silently or say aloud: "I am cleansing this space of any negativity or harmful energy and creating space for white light to shine through."

SMUDGING PERSONAL ENERGY

The same rules apply when looking to clear your own personal energy. Here's how:

1. Stand up straight with your feet firmly planted on the ground and take a few deep and centering breaths.
2. Once you feel calm and present, gently guide the smoke around your body from bottom to top (or from your root to your crown chakra).

This ritual can be done as often as you like. I find it very beneficial to do this after a stressful day or when experiencing anger or tension. This is something I often recommend for those who live their lives very publicly, do a lot of speaking engagements/performances, or find themselves around lots of different types of people and energy on a regular basis. Once you experience the benefits of smudging, your intuition will let you know when it's time to do it again.

13.

Crystal Essences and Elixirs

Thousands of years ago, the healers and OG beauticians of ancient civilizations utilized crystals and gems as part of their beauty regimens, as cures for ailments, to align energies, and for manifesting desires. Often in doing this, they would concoct elixirs and tonics, crush up stones into powders for the skin, and steep certain crystals in water to make what are today known as "essences." Crystal essences can be applied topically, ingested as a drink, used for your pets, and even fed to your plants. Many people all over the world utilize the healing energy of crystal essences to soothe a wide variety of ailments—from constipation, to cuts/wounds, to wrinkles. It can be fun to make note of the differences you start to feel!

Just like the stones themselves, each crystal essence has a specific vibrational energy. By using an essence, you allow the healing properties of the crystal it's made from to work on you from the inside out. In this chapter, you will learn what a crystal essence is, how to use them, and how to make them.

WHAT ARE CRYSTAL ESSENCES AND ELIXIRS?

Using a crystal essence is an amazing way to deepen your crystal healing practice and experience its benefits from the inside out. When you charge your water with a healing crystal by steeping it for several hours (almost like a tea), you are transferring some of its energy directly into the water. These concoctions can be made with water to drink (usually called an elixir) or with carrier oils to put on your skin (usually called an essence). For simplicity, I've called them essences in this chapter.

Water is an extremely programmable substance (check out the work of Dr. Masaru Emoto when you get a chance), and it takes on the vibrational frequency of the stones that you immerse in it. That's why pairing the energy of crystals with water is so effective. Making and using crystal essences can be a very powerful addition to your current crystal healing routine!

USES FOR CRYSTAL ESSENCES

As with everything else in the crystal world, you want to determine and state your intentions and then surrender and go with the flow. Using a crystal essence is incredibly easy and can be a great alternative to actually having to carry your crystals with you. Once you have made your desired crystal essence (which we will go over next), you can use it as:

* Drinking water to stay hydrated
* A bath additive
* Under-the-tongue drops (as many holistic substances are taken—the top of your tongue has taste buds that can affect taste and absorption, so under the tongue is a more efficient way)
* A refresher spray for face or body
* A room spray
* A skin treatment applied by hand or with a cotton pad

See—simple, right?!

TYPES OF CRYSTAL ESSENCE LIQUIDS

When it comes to making crystal essences or elixirs, you can use water or oil. When you use a carrier oil, it is best to use the resulting essence as a skin or hair treatment that is absorbed topically. Here's what you need to know:

* **Carrier Oil:** The oil you choose to make your essence with is referred to as a "carrier oil" and should always be in the form of a cold-pressed vegetable oil. Depending on where you will be using this oil (face vs. body), you will choose between either a heavy or a light oil. It's totally dependent on personal preference. (I have oilier skin naturally, so I go with lighter oils.) Carrier oil essence will stay energetically fresh anywhere from six months to one year, depending on the oil. Check the expiration date on your oil of choice before using it to make your essence.
  * **Lighter Oils:** Apricot kernel, evening primrose, grape seed, jojoba, safflower, sesame
  * **Heavier Oils:** Avocado, coconut, olive oil, sweet almond, sunflower, vitamin E, walnut
* **Water:** Use only spring, distilled, or alkaline water. Water essences can last a few days by themselves. If any preservatives (such as apple cider vinegar, vodka, or brandy) are added, they will stay fresh for a few weeks.

WHAT YOU'LL NEED BEFORE YOU START

Though making crystal essence is incredibly easy, you will still need to be prepared before you begin. Here are items to have on hand as you get started:

* A glass vessel (think mason jar, carafe, milk bottle, or large drinking glass).

* Additional containers like a glass spray bottle or dropper to house the essence in (dependent solely on your preference).
* Glass stopper or glass lid. You can also use cheesecloth or organic cotton fabric with a rubber band (this prevents debris from falling into your essence as it sets).
* Water (natural spring, distilled, or alkaline) or carrier oil.
* Crystals (use only tumbled stones to prevent any breakage or residue from remaining in the essence).
* Preservative liquid. Apple cider vinegar (ACV), vodka, or brandy are some top choices. (These preservative liquids are only necessary for use in water essences to prolong shelf life if you plan to keep them longer than a few days. They're not necessary for carrier oil essences.)
* Wooden or glass spoon to immerse and remove the stone. Do not place metal, plastic, or even your own skin into the liquid so as not to disturb or taint the energy of the entire batch.
* Pen and masking tape or label (to name your batch).
* Intention (What is the intention you want to set on the healing properties of this essence? What do you want to manifest in your spirit or life?).

Important: Make sure all items are clean and sterile.

IMPORTANT CAUTIONS

It is very important to note which crystals can be toxic when added to water or which may disintegrate/become ruined when soaked in water for long periods. Here is a list of the crystals covered in this book that should NOT be used when making crystal essences. Beyond this list, please be super diligent in doing your own research on any stones that are not covered in these pages before you use them for any future essence creations.

Do not use the following crystals when making essences:

amazonite, aquamarine, black tourmaline, bloodstone, chrysocolla, fluorite, gold tektite, hematite, jade, kyanite, labradorite, lapis lazuli, lepidolite, malachite, moldavite, moonstone, pyrite, red garnet, ruby, selenite, serpentine, shattuckite, smoky quartz, tangerine quartz, tiger's eye, turquoise, watermelon tourmaline

Though there are a lot of exciting stones listed above that are a big no-no when it comes to these recipes (bummer!), I've got some good news for you. Although those specific crystals cannot be directly immersed in your elixir water, there is a way around it, and it's as easy as finding another glass cup or bottle. Your crystals do not need to make direct contact with the water in order to transfer their vibrational energy into the water (kind of like how we don't have to implant crystals into our bodies in order to receive their healing energy). Place the stone you would like to work with in a small glass cup, bottle, or container that is sized so that it can fit within the glass vessel housing your water. Then proceed like normal, removing the glassed crystal once you are done with the recipe.

HOW TO MAKE CRYSTAL ESSENCES

Making crystal essences is extremely easy and can also be very fun! I will go over some recipes in just a few pages, but for now, here are the basic steps needed to begin making your own crystal essence at home.

* Pick your crystal. (Use only one or two types of stones per essence your first few times. Later, when you have more experience, you can mix different essences together if you wish.)

* Make sure your crystal is physically cleansed of any dirt, bacteria, or grime using a natural soap and distilled water. Dry with a cloth. (If your crystal can't be immersed in water, rinse quickly and wipe dry immediately.)
* Get into a relaxed and calm state of mind before you begin. I like to meditate for several moments while seated before creating my essence.
* Energetically clear and charge your crystal (see Chapter 2).
* Fill your glass vessel with 16 ounces of water or carrier oil and immerse your crystal in it.
* Set your positive intention for this healing crystal essence (using the steps from Chapter 2).
* Label the glass vessel with your positive intention, the crystals used, and the date created.
* Cover the liquid and let it sit in direct sunlight or moonlight. Water needs to charge for 7 hours while carrier oil should charge for 24. (If you do not have access to direct sunlight, use faux sunlight by getting a full-spectrum lightbulb—but try for the real thing.)
* If adding a preservative liquid to your water essence (ACV, vodka, or brandy) use the 60/40 rule (60 percent of vessel filled with essence, 40 percent with preservative liquid) and do it only after your essence has charged. Once you add a preservative to your essence, the batch should only be used as drops under the tongue or as drops added to drinking water. Do not drink this straight because of the high alcohol/ACV content.
* Refrigerate when not in use.

CRYSTAL ESSENCE RECIPES

Part of the fun of working with crystal essences is coming up with all sorts of creative and powerful concoctions! I will now share some of my favorite essence recipes. As you build your collection, you will add your own to the mix!

ESSENCE FOR LOVE

This essence is all about attracting more moments of love and kindness into your life. Love can manifest itself in many ways, and whether it's a romance or kindred friendship, we could all use an extra dose of it sometimes, right? Using this essence will help you experience spontaneous moments of care, compassion, and kindness as you move through your day. Rose quartz powerfully draws love toward you and turquoise brings an energy of wholeness and confidence to your life. This particular essence makes for a perfect additive to your perfume or lotion by simply placing a few drops of carrier oil essence into your hand as you smooth the lotion over your body (or dab a couple drops on your wrists or behind your ears after spraying perfume).

INGREDIENTS

* Rose quartz and turquoise (Because turquoise is water soluble and can be toxic, place it in a separate, small, sealed glass vessel before placing it into the liquid.)
* 1 glass vessel
* 1 sterilized glass dropper or spray bottle (optional)
* 1 wooden spoon
* 16 ounces water or carrier oil
* 4–8 ounces preservative liquid (optional for water essence only)
* Sunlight or moonlight

1. Fill your sterilized glass vessel with 16 ounces of water or carrier oil.
2. Gently place crystals into liquid with wooden spoon.
3. Set your intention upon the essence by saying aloud: "The intention I am setting on the healing crystal essence is _____. I will use its powerful energy to release what no longer serves me and to grow my highest self." Be thoughtful and specific as you do this.
4. Place in direct sunlight or moonlight (7 hours for water, 24 for carrier oil).
5. Remove crystals with your wooden spoon and place to the side.
6. Add in a 60/40 ratio of preservative (optional).
7. Fill glass dropper/spray bottle with essence to begin using immediately (optional).
8. Label and date your glass vessel and bottle (optional).
9. Store the essence in the refrigerator until needed.

———◆———

MANTRA

I attract and gift to others the energy

of kindness and love.

ESSENCE FOR SOOTHING

This essence for soothing is perfect for women who experience painful cramping and emotional restlessness during their menstruation. By utilizing the healing energy of moonstone, which is a very cyclical stone (meaning that its energy has been thought to move with the cycles of the moon, for which it is also named) known for its goddess energy, and lapis lazuli, which is a powerful tool for inner peace and mental stamina, this essence will bring you pain relief and a stabilizing connection between your emotional and mental selves. Add to your drinking water (remember, only drink water essences) or gently massage the oil version on your lower back and stomach.

INGREDIENTS

* Moonstone and lapis lazuli (Because lapis lazuli is water soluble and can be toxic, place it in a small, sealed, separate glass vessel before putting it into the liquid.)
* 1 glass vessel
* 1 sterilized glass dropper or spray bottle
* 1 wooden spoon
* 16 ounces water or carrier oil
* 4–8 ounces preservative liquid (optional for water essence only)
* Sunlight or moonlight

1. Fill your sterilized glass vessel with 16 ounces of water or carrier oil.
2. Gently place crystals into liquid with wooden spoon.

3. Set your intention upon the essence by saying aloud: "The intention I am setting on the healing crystal essence is _____. I will use its powerful energy to release what no longer serves me and to grow my highest self." Be thoughtful and specific as you do this.

4. Place in direct sunlight or moonlight (7 hours for water, 24 for carrier oil).

5. Remove crystals with your wooden spoon and place to the side.

6. Add in a 60/40 ratio of preservative (optional).

7. Fill glass dropper/spray bottle with essence to begin using immediately (optional).

8. Label and date your glass vessel and bottle (optional).

9. Store the essence in the refrigerator until needed.

MANTRA

I am embracing my inner goddess and surrender

to the power of the divine.

ESSENCE FOR EMOTIONAL HEALING

This essence for emotional healing is wonderful for those looking to have emotional freedom and release any energy that has kept them bound to painful, unfair, and harmful experiences. The energy of amethyst will help break through deeply programmed emotional patterns while kyanite will lend itself to manifesting a shift in your perception of the world and things that you have experienced while also clearing away blockages. Add this essence to your drinking water (remember, only drink water essences) or give yourself a loving closed-eyes massage with the oil version.

INGREDIENTS
* Amethyst and kyanite
* 1 glass vessel
* 1 sterilized glass dropper or spray bottle
* 1 wooden spoon
* 16 ounces spring, distilled, or alkaline water or carrier oil
* 4–8 ounces preservative liquid (apple cider vinegar, vodka, or brandy)
* Sunlight or moonlight

1. Fill your sterilized glass vessel with 16 ounces of water or carrier oil.
2. Gently place crystals into liquid with wooden spoon.

3. Set your intention upon the essence by saying aloud: "The intention I am setting on the healing crystal essence is _____. I will use its powerful energy to release what no longer serves me and to grow my highest self." Be thoughtful and specific as you do this.
4. Place in direct sunlight or moonlight (7 hours for water, 24 for carrier oil).
5. Add in a 60/40 ratio of preservative (optional).
6. Remove crystals with your wooden spoon and place to the side.
7. Fill glass dropper/spray bottle with essence to begin using immediately (optional).
8. Label and date your glass vessel and bottle (optional).
9. Store the essence in the refrigerator until needed.

MANTRA

I open my heart to complete emotional healing and transformation.

ESSENCE FOR VITAL ENERGY

This essence for vital energy is great for a pick-me-up and motivation when you find yourself feeling a little sluggish or lazy. Carnelian is an energizing stone that encourages vitality, bold action, and sexuality while shiva lingam is beloved for its "kundalini" (primal, sacred energy) activation abilities that bring strength and balance to the entire body. This is great for under-the-tongue drops or as an additive to your drinking water when working out.

INGREDIENTS
* Carnelian and shiva lingam
* 1 glass vessel
* 1 sterilized glass dropper or spray bottle
* 1 wooden spoon
* 16 ounces spring, distilled, or alkaline water or carrier oil
* 4–8 ounces preservative liquid (apple cider vinegar, vodka, or brandy)
* Sunlight or moonlight

1. Fill your sterilized glass vessel with 16 ounces of water or carrier oil.
2. Gently place crystals into liquid with wooden spoon.
3. Set your intention upon the essence by saying aloud: "The intention I am setting on the healing crystal essence is _____. I will use its powerful energy to release what no longer serves me and to grow my highest self." Be thoughtful and specific as you do this.

4. Place in direct sunlight or moonlight (7 hours for water, 24 for carrier oil).
5. Add in a 60/40 ratio of preservative (optional).
6. Remove crystals with your wooden spoon and place to the side.
7. Fill glass dropper/spray bottle with essence to begin using immediately (optional).
8. Label and date your glass vessel and bottle (optional).
9. Store the essence in the refrigerator until needed.

MANTRA

My body is strong and my mind is alert.

ESSENCE FOR FORGIVENESS

This essence for forgiveness will provide gentle and compassionate healing energy to help you move forward in your emotional healing and spiritual growth. The ability to forgive lies in being able to express a level of compassion and divine understanding to those who have harmed you, and even to those who do not seek your forgiveness. Chrysoprase aids in helping you see the deeper karmic lessons in your life's experiences and supports your heart in staying open, while spirit quartz is a powerful tool for facilitating your spiritual evolution so you may live as your highest self.

INGREDIENTS

* Chrysoprase and spirit quartz (Because chrysoprase can be toxic, place it in a small, separate, sealed glass vessel before putting it into the liquid. Because toxicity is dependent on what type of spirit quartz you use, it is best to use a sealed glass vessel for it as well.)
* 1 glass vessel
* 1 sterilized glass dropper or spray bottle
* 1 wooden spoon
* 16 ounces spring, distilled, or alkaline water or carrier oil
* 4–8 ounces preservative liquid (apple cider vinegar, vodka, or brandy)
* Sunlight or moonlight

1. Fill your sterilized glass vessel with 16 ounces of water or carrier oil.
2. Gently place crystals into liquid with wooden spoon.

3. Set your intention upon the essence by saying aloud: "The intention I am setting on the healing crystal essence is _____. I will use its powerful energy to release what no longer serves me and to grow my highest self." Be thoughtful and specific as you do this.
4. Place in direct sunlight or moonlight (7 hours for water, 24 for carrier oil).
5. Remove crystals with your wooden spoon and place to the side.
6. Add in a 60/40 ratio of preservative (optional).
7. Fill glass dropper/spray bottle with essence to begin using immediately (optional).
8. Label and date your glass vessel and bottle (optional).
9. Store the essence in the refrigerator until needed.

MANTRA

In forgiving others, I also forgive myself.

ESSENCE FOR SUCCESS

This essence for success is the perfect additive to use if you are looking to manifest opportunity, abundance, and important relationships. Red garnet has long been prized for its ability to help others see you in a more attractive and irresistible light, while citrine, also known as the "stone of success," has the vibrational power to lead you toward opportune moments and experiences. Use this essence as an addition to your lotions, body creams, or perfumes.

INGREDIENTS

* Red garnet and citrine (Because red garnet can be toxic, place it in a small, separate, sealed glass vessel before putting it into the liquid.)
* 1 glass vessel
* 1 sterilized glass dropper or spray bottle
* 1 wooden spoon
* 16 ounces spring, distilled, or alkaline water or carrier oil
* 4–8 ounces preservative liquid (apple cider vinegar, vodka, or brandy)
* Sunlight or moonlight

1. Fill your sterilized glass vessel with 16 ounces of water or carrier oil.
2. Gently place crystals into liquid with wooden spoon.
3. Set your intention upon the essence by saying aloud: "The intention I am setting on the healing crystal essence is _____. I will

use its powerful energy to release what no longer serves me and to grow my highest self." Be thoughtful and specific as you do this.

4. Place in direct sunlight or moonlight (7 hours for water, 24 for carrier oil).
5. Remove crystals with your wooden spoon and place to the side.
6. Add in a 60/40 ratio of preservative (optional).
7. Fill glass dropper/spray bottle with essence to begin using immediately (optional).
8. Label and date your glass vessel and bottle (optional).
9. Store the essence in the refrigerator until needed.

MANTRA

I attract opportunity and success into my life.

ESSENCE FOR CREATIVITY

This essence for creativity will be a powerful ally for accessing the most innovative parts of your thoughts and stimulating a free flow of ideas. The energy it emits will help you unlock your unlimited potential to create. Mookaite jasper, a highly intuitive stone, will amplify your own instincts for clear decision-making and works harmoniously with pyrite, which is notorious for unlocking your personal power of manifestation by stimulating your ideas and moving you toward taking action. Place water essence drops into your drinking water several times a day.

INGREDIENTS
* Mookaite and pyrite (Because pyrite can be toxic, place it in a small, separate, sealed glass vessel before putting it into the liquid.)
* 1 glass vessel
* 1 sterilized glass dropper or spray bottle
* 1 wooden spoon
* 16 ounces spring, distilled, or alkaline water or carrier oil
* 4–8 ounces preservative liquid (apple cider vinegar, vodka, or brandy)
* Sunlight or moonlight

1. Fill your sterilized glass vessel with 16 ounces of water or carrier oil.
2. Gently place crystals into liquid with wooden spoon.
3. Set your intention upon the essence by saying aloud: "The intention I am setting on the healing crystal essence is _____. I will

use its powerful energy to release what no longer serves me and to grow my highest self." Be thoughtful and specific as you do this.

4. Place in direct sunlight or moonlight (7 hours for water, 24 for carrier oil).
5. Remove crystals with your wooden spoon and place to the side.
6. Add in a 60/40 ratio of preservative (optional).
7. Fill glass dropper/spray bottle with essence to begin using immediately (optional).
8. Label and date your glass vessel and bottle (optional).
9. Store the essence in the refrigerator until needed.

MANTRA

I confidently use my imagination to create a reality of infinite possibilities.

ESSENCE FOR GOOD HEALTH

This essence for good health is perfect for promoting healthy living and physical healing. Shattuckite is thought to be an aid for general good health and is often used in elixirs and tonics because it can be very successful treating minor colds and providing balance for acidity in the body. Shungite, an ancient healing stone that has existed for billions of years on earth, is the only natural source of fullerenes (a powerful antioxidant) and energetically, it's believed that anything that can be a hazard to human health cannot exist when shungite is present. This water essence is perfect for daily use via drops under the tongue or added to your drinking water or tea.

INGREDIENTS

* Shungite and shattuckite (Because shattuckite can be toxic, place it in a small, separate, sealed glass vessel before putting it into the liquid.)
* 1 glass vessel
* 1 sterilized glass dropper or spray bottle
* 1 wooden spoon
* 16 ounces spring, distilled, or alkaline water or carrier oil
* 4–8 ounces preservative liquid (apple cider vinegar, vodka, or brandy)
* Sunlight or moonlight

1. Fill your sterilized glass vessel with 16 ounces of water or carrier oil.
2. Gently place crystals into liquid with wooden spoon.

3. Set your intention upon the essence by saying aloud: "The intention I am setting on the healing crystal essence is _____. I will use its powerful energy to release what no longer serves me and to grow my highest self." Be thoughtful and specific as you do this.
4. Place in direct sunlight or moonlight (7 hours for water, 24 for carrier oil).
5. Remove crystals with your wooden spoon and place to the side.
6. Add in a 60/40 ratio of preservative (optional).
7. Fill glass dropper/spray bottle with essence to begin using immediately (optional).
8. Label and date your glass vessel and bottle (optional).
9. Store the essence in the refrigerator until needed.

MANTRA

My body is in perfect alignment and heals easily.

ESSENCE FOR HAPPINESS

This essence for happiness makes a wonderful daily companion for experiencing enhanced joy and feelings of optimism and wholeness. Watermelon tourmaline connects you to a larger understanding of happiness by helping you find joy in all moments (even the difficult ones), and ruby is a high-vibrating gem that carries an energy of fierce passion and exuberant enthusiasm. This blend of crystals encourages an ease of mind and a zest for living. Add water essence to your drinking water or gently massage your heart space with an infused carrier oil.

INGREDIENTS

* Watermelon tourmaline and ruby (Because watermelon tourmaline and ruby crystals can be toxic, place them in small, separate, sealed glass vessels before putting them into the liquid.)
* 1 glass vessel
* 1 sterilized glass dropper or spray bottle
* 1 wooden spoon
* 16 ounces spring, distilled, or alkaline water or carrier oil
* 4–8 ounces preservative liquid (apple cider vinegar, vodka, or brandy)
* Sunlight or moonlight

1. Fill your sterilized glass vessel with 16 ounces of water or carrier oil.
2. Gently place crystals into liquid with wooden spoon.

3. Set your intention upon the essence by saying aloud: "The intention I am setting on the healing crystal essence is _____. I will use its powerful energy to release what no longer serves me and to grow my highest self." Be thoughtful and specific as you do this.

4. Place in direct sunlight or moonlight (7 hours for water, 24 for carrier oil).

5. Remove crystals with your wooden spoon and place to the side.

6. Add in a 60/40 ratio of preservative (optional).

7. Fill glass dropper/spray bottle with essence to begin using immediately (optional).

8. Label and date your glass vessel and bottle (optional).

9. Store the essence in the refrigerator until needed.

MANTRA

My heart is filled with gratitude and joyful optimism.

ESSENCE FOR PROTECTION

This essence for protection can work as a powerful tool to protect you—mind, body, and spirit. Black tourmaline is a dominant force that protects against negative or destructive people, as well as dark energy and entities. Labradorite, also known as the "stone of magic," helps preserve your personal energy and blocks people from being able to drain you. In addition, it covers you in a protective energy as you grow spiritually. Use this water essence via drops under the tongue as you see fit. It also makes for a wonderful room spray, especially after visitors and guests depart.

INGREDIENTS

* Black tourmaline and labradorite (Because black tourmaline and labradorite crystals can be toxic, place them in small, separate, sealed glass vessels before putting them into the liquid.)
* 1 glass vessel
* 1 sterilized glass dropper or spray bottle
* 1 wooden spoon
* 16 ounces spring, distilled, or alkaline water or carrier oil
* 4–8 ounces preservative liquid (apple cider vinegar, vodka, or brandy)
* Sunlight or moonlight

1. Fill your sterilized glass vessel with 16 ounces of water or carrier oil.
2. Gently place crystals into liquid with wooden spoon.

3. Set your intention upon the essence by saying aloud: "The intention I am setting on the healing crystal essence is _____. I will use its powerful energy to release what no longer serves me and to grow my highest self." Be thoughtful and specific as you do this.

4. Place in direct sunlight or moonlight (7 hours for water, 24 for carrier oil).

5. Remove crystals with your wooden spoon and place to the side.

6. Add in a 60/40 ratio of preservative (optional).

7. Fill glass dropper/spray bottle with essence to begin using immediately (optional).

8. Label and date your glass vessel and bottle (optional).

9. Store the essence in the refrigerator until needed.

MANTRA

I am being divinely protected and feel safe and secure.

ESSENCE FOR BALANCE

This essence for balance is a gentle but powerful addition to your daily wellness routine. Clear quartz, also known as "the universal stone," is a crystal prized for its balancing energy. It is connected to all the chakras and when used as an essence and in meditation, it can help balance each one of your seven chakra points. Blue lace agate has a beautiful ability to unburden the mind and create a soothing energy for any feelings of anxiety or overstimulation. When clear quartz and blue lace agate are used together, you will begin to experience more feelings of alignment, balance, and calm. Use this water essence via drops under the tongue as you see fit. It also makes for a great facial misting spray.

INGREDIENTS

* Clear quartz and blue lace agate
* 1 glass vessel
* 1 sterilized glass dropper or spray bottle
* 1 wooden spoon
* 16 ounces spring, distilled, or alkaline water or carrier oil
* 4–8 ounces preservative liquid (apple cider vinegar, vodka, or brandy)
* Sunlight or moonlight

1. Fill your sterilized glass vessel with 16 ounces of water or carrier oil.
2. Gently place crystals into liquid with wooden spoon.

3. Set your intention upon the essence by saying aloud: "The intention I am setting on the healing crystal essence is _____. I will use its powerful energy to release what no longer serves me and to grow my highest self." Be thoughtful and specific as you do this.
4. Place in direct sunlight or moonlight (7 hours for water, 24 for carrier oil).
5. Remove crystals with your wooden spoon and place to the side.
6. Add in a 60/40 ratio of preservative (optional).
7. Fill glass dropper/spray bottle with essence to begin using immediately (optional).
8. Label and date your glass vessel and bottle (optional).
9. Store the essence in the refrigerator until needed.

MANTRA

I am being divinely protected and feel balanced and secure.

14.

Crystals and Chakras

Throughout this book, I have shared dozens of profiles of beautiful and energetic healing crystals. In each entry, you probably saw a note about which chakra is associated with each of the stones. Now, you may have been reading those thinking, "What the heck is she talking about?" or you could be on the other end of the spectrum and already be familiar with the term and the practice. Either way, working with your chakras can be a very powerful experience and pretty exciting!

I'll never forget the very first time I began to understand what my chakras were and how they worked. Though I had leafed through a few books and seen diagrams (usually a man seated with legs crossed and a bunch of different circle spots lined up on his body), I really had no idea what the fuss was all about. Then two things that felt pretty life-changing happened: I was led through a chakra meditation while on a retreat, and I experienced a chakra healing firsthand. After that moment (which I will go into more detail about in this chapter), meditating with crystals on my chakra points became a mainstay within my spiritual practice.

In this chapter, I will give you an overview on what "chakra" actually means, where they are and how to use your crystals with them to enhance your personal power and quality of life. It's officially time to dig even deeper into this energy journey and manifest some free-flowing energy in all areas!

WHAT ARE CHAKRAS?

The word *chakra* itself (pronounced "cha"-"kra") comes from a Sanskrit word meaning "wheel," "circle," and "cycle." The word is usually translated as "a spinning wheel of light and energy." Sanskrit is an ancient (4,000 or so years old!) Indian language often used in Hinduism and Buddhism.

So far in this book we have talked a lot about energy. As human beings, we are made of energy. The crystals we use are made of energy and every single thing on this planet and in the universe is made of energy. Our chakras are wheels of extremely powerful energy that exist inside of our bodies and are constantly spinning. Though there are thought to be several thousand minor chakras in our bodies, seven are considered to be the most powerful. These seven main chakras are what we study and work with in crystal healing, yoga, meditation, and Ayurveda.

The main seven chakras that each of us have are aligned within our bodies from the base of our spines to the top of our heads. So if you can imagine, picture seven separate wheels that are radiating energy and light, going in a straight line from your head down along your spine to your tailbone. Those chakras regulate the flow of energy that moves throughout our bodies and make up what is called our "energy system."

When I was studying meditation, my guru once described chakras as being like invisible human batteries. They are what power us, and they, like batteries, need to be recharged. In the case of chakras, they need to be recharged by cosmic energy and cleared when needed. Sometimes, due to life and the complicated nature of being alive in this world, we may experience blockages in our energy system. These blockages look kind of like a pipe that is clogged in different places. When we have blockages in our chakras and energy is unable to flow freely, we experience problems that can manifest as physical, mental, emotional, or spiritual. In order to lead a healthy and balanced life, we must work to keep our energy channels clear.

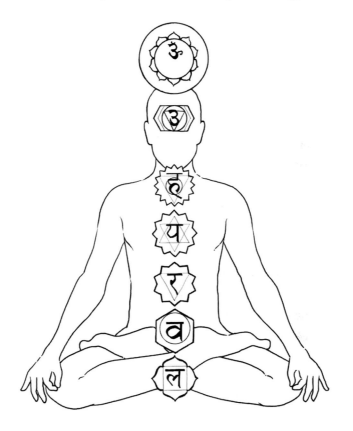

The seven major chakras in the body. From the top down, the chakra points are: crown, third eye, throat, heart, solar plexus, sacral, and root.

If you think you may be experiencing blocked energy in your chakras, utilize your healing crystals to do some balancing and clearing work on yourself as you meditate. Coming up in the next few pages of this chapter,

I will share more detail on each of your seven chakras and which crystals they correlate with.

WHAT IS CHAKRA HEALING?

Blockages in this powerful energy system that is pulsing through us can cause a range of issues, from aches and pains to stress and anxiety. When this happens, it is important for us to clear those blockages through chakra healing.

So what exactly is chakra healing? Well, chakra healing is when you take stock of the energy levels of your chakras and heal areas where there is distress or blockages by one of the following means:

* Chakra healing with crystals
* Energy work (Reiki)
* Balancing massage with aromatherapy
* Yoga
* Chakra sound healing
* Chakra meditation with mantras/affirmations

By doing one of or several of these things, you are able to balance, cleanse, and heal your chakras to restore the flow of energy that radiates along your spine through your body. When your chakras are in perfect condition, you are able to experience great mental, physical, emotional, and spiritual health.

Years ago as I was beginning my meditation and crystal journey, I attended a retreat that left me deeply changed. Up until that time I had a vague familiarity with what chakras were but did not really integrate them into my spiritual routine. On the third day of the retreat, my guru led us in a special chakra meditation. As I sat with my eyes closed in a room with roughly one hundred other people, I envisioned my chakra points lighting up one by one and chanted their Sanskrit names silently. As I did that, I was able to go deeper into my meditation practice than I ever had and felt a significant energy shift in my body. Later that day, I was blessed with experiencing an incredible chakra healing at the hands of a goddess named Jennifer that made me feel like I had literally left my body and looked down at myself while floating. At the beginning of the day I had felt like I was filled with stagnated energy—very sluggish and out of balance. When the day came to an end, I felt more energetically charged and open than I'd ever felt in my life. I smiled with all my teeth, hands raised in gratitude, and wept happy tears all the way back to my room.

CRYSTALS FOR YOUR CHAKRAS

Though there are said to be thousands of invisible chakras that reside within your body, in crystal healing, yoga, meditation, and Ayurveda, only seven are considered to be of primary importance. Every chakra has specific healing crystals that they resonate strongly with and that can be used as tools to clear any blockages they may get. You will even notice that many of the crystals used for specific chakras tend to be the same color that's associated with that chakra. In this section, we will go over the names and makeup of those seven beautiful wheels of cosmic energy and which crystals in your collection you can use with them!

1ST CHAKRA

Root

Your first chakra is known as the root chakra and is located at the base of your spine.

* **Color:** Red
* **Sanskrit Name:** Muladhara
* **Function:** Grounding, stability, and security

CRYSTALS FOR THIS CHAKRA

Use these crystals for any healing work that you do with this chakra.

* Hematite
* Mookaite
* Smoky quartz

MANTRA

I am strong and deeply rooted to the earth.

2ND CHAKRA

Sacral

Your second chakra is known as the sacral chakra and is located between your navel and your genital area.

* **Color:** Orange
* **Sanskrit Name:** Svadhisthana
* **Function:** Sexuality, relationships, and emotions

CRYSTALS FOR THIS CHAKRA

Use these crystals for any healing work that you do with this chakra.

* Carnelian
* Moonstone
* Citrine

MANTRA

I have creative energy flowing freely through my body.

3RD CHAKRA

Solar Plexus

Your third chakra is known as the solar plexus chakra and is located at your navel.

* **Color:** Yellow
* **Sanskrit Name:** Manipura
* **Function:** Vitality and life-force energy

CRYSTALS FOR THIS CHAKRA

Use these crystals for any healing work that you do with this chakra.

* Malachite
* Citrine
* Tiger's eye

MANTRA

*I am bold and confident in action
and attract much success.*

4TH CHAKRA

Heart

Your fourth chakra is known as the heart chakra and is located at your heart.

* **Color:** Green
* **Sanskrit Name:** Anahata
* **Function:** Love, compassion, and balance

CRYSTALS FOR THIS CHAKRA

Use these crystals for any healing work that you do with this chakra.

* Watermelon tourmaline
* Rose quartz
* Green aventurine

MANTRA

I freely give and receive the energy of love.

5TH CHAKRA

Throat

Your fifth chakra is known as the throat chakra and is located at your throat.

* **Color:** Blue
* **Sanskrit Name:** Vishuddha
* **Function:** Communication, truth, and healing

CRYSTALS FOR THIS CHAKRA

Use these crystals for any healing work that you do with this chakra.

* Blue lace agate
* Turquoise
* Aquamarine

MANTRA

I express myself with truth and compassion.

6TH CHAKRA

Third Eye

Your sixth chakra is known as the third eye chakra and is located at your forehead.

* **Color:** Indigo
* **Sanskrit Name:** Ajna
* **Function:** Intuition, wisdom, and understanding

CRYSTALS FOR THIS CHAKRA

Use these crystals for any healing work that you do with this chakra.

* Lapis lazuli
* Amethyst
* Moldavite

MANTRA

I call on divine wisdom for a deeper understanding of my experiences.

7TH CHAKRA

Crown

Your seventh chakra is known as the crown chakra and is located at the top of your head.

* **Color:** Violet
* **Sanskrit Name:** Sahasrara
* **Function:** Enlightenment and cosmic consciousness

CRYSTALS FOR THIS CHAKRA

Use these crystals for any healing work that you do with this chakra.

* Labradorite
* Spirit quartz
* Selenite

MANTRA

I am one with the universe.

EPILOGUE

Now that we have reached the end of this *Crystal Bliss* adventure, I hope you choose to walk into this new journey of spirit with an open mind and an open heart.

Though it can be tempting, there is no need to rush out and collect every crystal you see. Start slow by buying a few stones that really resonate with you. Keep them near as often as possible, meditate with them, and then go from there. When it comes to the growth of the self, the process takes as long as it is meant to take, so instead of rushing yourself, work on being more present in each moment and just thoughtfully enjoy the ride.

Working with crystals and practicing meditation has added so much balance and beautiful energy to my life. Personally, professionally, and spiritually, I feel as if I am living a more purposeful, present, and joyful life all around. I am now so excited for you to begin to experience that same energy in your own life!

You can connect with me personally on social media via:

@DeviBrown on *Twitter*, *Instagram*, and *Facebook*

...and you can check out some of my Karma Bliss crystals at:

KarmaBliss.com or @KarmaBlissed on *Instagram*

I would love to hear from you. Namaste!

INDEX